A Beginner's Guide

Dendrobium bracteosum

A Beginner's Guide

John Mason

HYLAND HOUSE

First published in Australia in 2001 by
Hyland House Publishing Pty Ltd
PO Box 122
Flemington
Victoria 3031

National Library of Australia
Cataloguing-in-publication data:

Mason, John, 1951-.
Orchids: a beginner's guide.
Includes index.
ISBN 1 86447 084 4.
1. Orchids. 2. Orchid culture – Australia. I. Title.
635.9344

Edited by Bet Moore
Design & layout by Captured Concepts
Printed by Shannon Books, Melbourne

Contents

OTHER BOOKS BY JOHN MASON:

Growing Australian Natives (1997), Kangaroo Press, Australia

Growing Conifers (1999), Kangaroo Press, Australia

Growing Ferns (1990), Kangaroo Press, Australia

Growing Pelargoniums & Geraniums, by Stockton, Stockton & Mason (1996) Hyland House, Australia

Growing Trees & Shrubs for Small Gardens (2000), Kangaroo Press, Australia

Growing Tropical Plants (1997), Kangaroo Press, Australia

Growing Vegetables (2nd edn) by Mason & Lawrence (1999), Kangaroo Press, Australia

Starting a Nursery or Herb Farm (1997), Kangaroo Press, Australia

Tropical & Warm Climate Gardening (1995), Bay Books, Australia

Nursery Management (1994), Kangaroo Press, Australia

Acknowledgments

The following staff from the Australian Correspondence Schools have contributed to this book:

Iain Harrison Dip.Hort.Sc.
Paul Plant B.App.Sc. (Hort.Tech.)
Cathy Travis B.Sc.Ag., Ass.App.Sc.

Thanks also to Gary Yong Gee who supplied advice on selected orchid species.
Photographs courtesy of John Mason and Gary Yong Gee
Line drawings by Stephen Mason

Page 1: (photo by Gary Yong Gee): *Brassavola nodosa*
Front cover: *Cymbidium* Autumn Green Mallow Green
Back cover top: *Zygopetalum intermedium*
Back cover bottom, left to right (photos by Gary Yong Gee): *Masdevillea polysticta*, *Laelia purpurata*, and *Rhyncholaelia digbyana*

An Introduction to Orchid Growing

What are orchids?

There are between 20,000 and 30,000 known orchid species, originating from almost every corner of the world. In fact, the only locations that are not home to at least one orchid species are the driest arid zones, and the Arctic and Antarctic.

Some orchids are valued for their commercial properties, but most are admired solely for their unique beauty. With so many orchids to choose from, every gardener has the opportunity to grow this lovely plant, no matter what their situation.

Orchid flowers are as diverse as the plants themselves, ranging from small and almost inconspicuous blooms to large, long-lasting flowers and flower stems. Some types of orchid are known to flower and provide colour for up to two months.

If your locality suits your choice of orchids, they are easy plants to grow, requiring very little attention once they are established in a favourable environment. This doesn't mean they'll thrive on neglect, just that they'll survive neglect better than orchids that are not suited to that situation.

The best approach to growing a particular orchid is to find out about its natural habitat, and try to recreate similar conditions.

In cool areas, most species will need protection from extreme cold, whilst in hot climates protection from direct sunlight is essential. For this reason, shadehouses and well-ventilated greenhouses are frequently used for orchid growing.

Orchids also perform well as pot plants, and are an attractive addition to ferneries and palm plantings.

Cool climate orchids include *Cymbidium*, *Dendrobium* and *Pleione* species, while *Dendrobium*, *Vanda* and *Cattleya* are good choices for warm areas. But with the right microclimate and good management, the possibilities are endless.

Economic value of orchids

The climbing genus *Vanilla* (mainly *Vanilla planiflora*) is the source of vanilla flavouring (from the pods).

Tubers from some genera (e.g. *Orchis*, *Dactylorhiza* and *Eulophia*) are used in a dried form in parts of Europe and Asia for medicinal and culinary purposes.

Many other genera are significant as ornamental plants, greenhouse plants and cut flowers. The genus *Cattleya* is probably the most extensively cultivated worldwide. The genus *Cymbidium* is the most widely grown in southern Australia.

Orchid classification

Orchids belong to the Orchidaceae family, one of the largest flowering plant families, with 735 genera and 20,000 species. They are perennial herbaceous plants, normally terrestrial in temperate climates, or epiphytes in tropical climates. They are occasionally saprophytic (i.e. living on dead organic material).

The division of orchid families into sub-families has been difficult. Various authorities have recommended different classification systems, making it difficult to accept one system. Some have recommended six sub-families, others three. In fact, the tribes vary for different authorities. (For genera that are not covered in this book, see *100 Plant Families*, Hickey & King, Cambridge University Press.)

Orchid characteristics

Orchids consist of a perianth with six segments: three outer sepals and three inner petals, with the lower petal, the lip or labellum, different from the others in shape, size and colour. It is usually the showy part of the flower and can be quite elaborate. Some labella are rounded, bucket shaped or tongue-like. The lip is attached at the top of the flower but appears to spring from the bottom because of the way the flower twists. The two remaining petals, which are identical, are often the same as the sepals.

Flowers are normally borne on stalks known as peduncles. These inflorescences may carry one flower or as many as one hundred, or even more.

Although most orchids are hermaphrodites, having flowers of both sexes, fertilisation must come from another plant. The ovary is always inferior in its placement (i.e. below the point where the perianth unites with the flower), and does not fully develop until it is fertilised. After flower fertilisation, the fruit capsule is produced, and this can contain up to thousands of minute seeds. Once the capsule matures and dries, it splits open to release the seed, which is dispersed by the wind.

Orchids are monocotyledons, like grasses and most flowering bulbs (e.g. onion, daffodil and iris). All monocotyledons have parallel veins in the leaves and, when a seed germinates, only one leaf is developed at first.

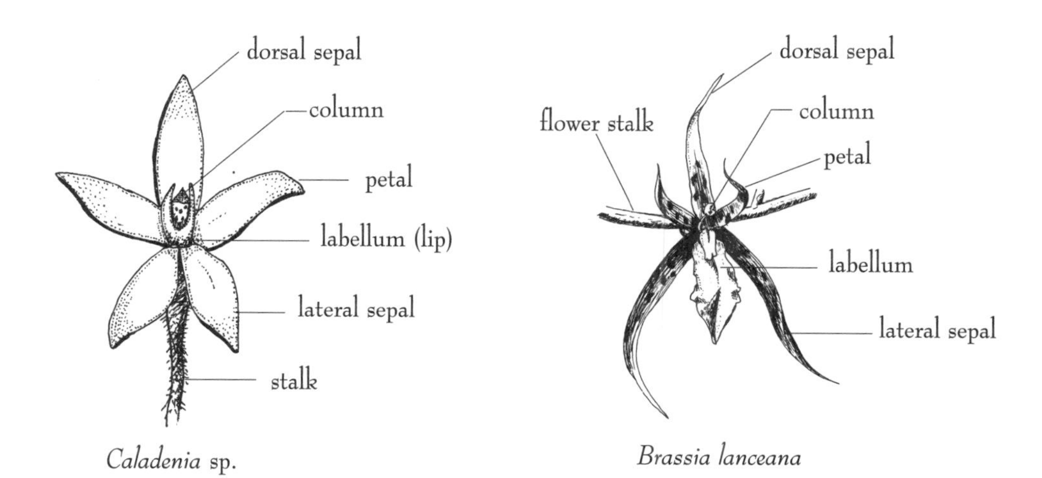

Caladenia sp.

Brassia lanceana

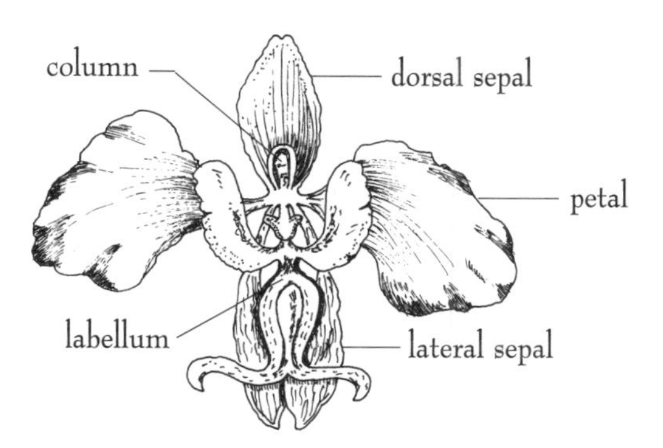

Phalaenopsis flower

GROWTH HABITS

Three main growth habits are distinguished:

- Sympodial: this refers to the horizontal growth habit of a creeping rhizome that produces periodic pseudostems (pseudobulbs) from lateral buds, e.g. *Dendrobium*, *Oncidium*, *Cattleya*.
- Monopodial: this means 'one foot' and refers to the upward growth habit. Some orchids, such as *Vanda* and *Ascocentrum*, have one growing tip and no rhizome or pseudostem.

- Geophytic: this refers to the swollen, root-like structures that help orchids survive drought and poor environmental conditions. These orchids tend to die down in the bad season and revive after environmental stimuli like rainfall or a change in temperature. This habit is predominantly associated with terrestrial orchids such as *Caladenia* and *Diuris*.

FOOD SOURCES

Orchids can be grouped according to the growing medium from which they feed:

- Epiphytic: these plants grow above ground, using another plant as a support, but not as a source of food (non-parasitic). They spread roots on the surface of trunks (or internally through crevices) to obtain nutrients in the rainwater as it trickles down the trunk. Tropical climate species of orchids are primarily epiphytic.
- Lithophytic: these plants grow on rocks. They normally obtain their sustenance from well-matted organic matter on or between the rocks.
- Terrestrial: like most other plants, these have a below-ground root system. Most cool climate orchids grow this way.

General guidelines for growing orchids

While some orchids require quite special growing conditions to achieve best results, the following general rules can be applied to many commonly grown orchids.

- Most orchids require a very loose open potting mix. This is commonly made from shredded or milled bark, or tree fern fibre.
- In cool climates, do not water orchids until the bark or fibre on the surface of the pot feels dry. Never let the entire pot dry out!
- When watering with a hose, keep the water jet soft and don't wash bark or fibre away from the roots.
- Don't water orchids with icy cold water. Generally make sure the water is at least 15°C. This may mean filling a watering can from your hose and, if it is a bit cold, adding some warmer water from a hot tap. Test as you go – be careful not to add too much hot water!
- Overwatering is more likely to kill an orchid than underwatering. Keep orchids relatively dry when growth is slow or dormant.
- Generally, the thicker the stem of the orchid (often called a pseudobulb) the less often the plant needs to be watered, unless conditions are very hot and dry.
- Avoid potting up orchids into too large a pot. Pot up a pot-bound plant into a pot only one or two pot sizes bigger each time, no more.
- Watch out for pests, in particular aphids, snails, scale or mealy bug insects, and use control methods as soon as they appear.

- Keep orchids in places where conditions remain fairly constant.
  - In cool climates, don't place them inside near an open window, where cold draughts could be a problem.
  - Keep them away from gas heaters or stoves.
  - Avoid an inside windowsill or bench where they will get direct (hot) sunlight. Most orchids prefer indirect light.
- Keep them out of the sun, particularly during the hottest part of the day, and generally provide shade in summer.
- Protect flower buds from direct sun, wind, aphids, snails and slugs.
- Do not overfeed. When in doubt, feed regularly with quarter-strength fertilisers.

Growing media

Naturally, the ideal growing medium is of enormous interest to orchid fanciers, who carry out extensive experiments to try to find the perfect medium for each different type of orchid. There are two main groups of orchids: epiphytic (and lithophytic) orchids and terrestrial (also known as geophytic) orchids.

Epiphytes grow on both living and dead (fallen) trees, and on the trunks of tree ferns. Lithophytes naturally grow on rocky outcrops. Terrestrial orchids have 'below ground' root systems.

Epiphytes can be grown on bark, cork or timber slabs. Placing epiphytic orchids directly onto existing trees has been a favourite technique for many successful growers. To increase your chances of success, it may be worth noting which plant the orchid attaches itself to in the wild – it may like *Casaurina*, for example, or it might favour *Melaleuca*.

The orchids should be securely tied to the slab or tree, avoiding damage to the plant, and ensuring that the roots are in direct contact with the medium (also called a substrate) they are tied to. The cork, bark or timber pieces can be fixed by simple wire hooks, or some other durable tying material, to walls or fences, or they can be hung from trees.

Many epiphytic orchids can also be grown successfully in pots. Both plastic and unglazed terracotta pots are suitable. The rather porous unglazed terracotta pots are especially suited to orchids that require good drainage. However, they are expensive, and can be fairly heavy to lift. Stakes should be used, particularly for taller species, to help minimise a plant's movement as this can easily damage the roots.

In general, it is best to use mostly inert materials for epiphytic orchids. Growers commonly use a potting mix that consists mainly of shredded or milled bark. A good mix is three parts medium-grade pine bark, one part shredded sphagnum moss, and one part perlite.

In Australia, national standards have been developed which specify the properties of potting mixes. Many excellent products that comply with these standards are commercially available. Debco Australia, for example, supplies three standard orchid mixes containing pine bark of three different degrees of coarseness.

Lithophytic orchids are usually grown in pots containing a mixture of both rock and bark material and most will adapt to the same cultural techniques used for epiphytic orchids.

Terrestrial orchids grow in the 'ground' — some actually grow in leaf litter, rather than the mineral soil beneath it. Some terrestrial orchids will also grow quite readily in soil-less mixes. Most terrestrial orchids can therefore be grown in mixes made up of composted bush debris, peat moss, medium to coarse sand, and small amounts of soil (generally representing only 15-20% of the mix). If the soil you are using is quite sandy then reduce the amount of added sand: the mix should not contain more than about 50% sand. Materials such as small gravel, charcoal, and perlite are sometimes added to help improve drainage.

Good aeration is important: you can allow the mix to almost dry out before watering.

MYCORRHIZA

There is a general consensus that orchids need various beneficial fungi in order to germinate, live and flower. Orchid seeds are unusual in that they contain only very small food reserves. When germination occurs this food reserve is rapidly used up, and if the orchid seed has no external food source it will soon die.

Recent studies have indicated that due to the orchids' ability to grow seeds in vitro, without fungi, this may not necessarily be true. However, since the presence of fungi in media is not harmful, there is no need to destroy them. Personal preference may decide the issue in the end.

If you decide in favour of fungi, the easiest way to acquire them for newly potted specimens is to remove one or two roots from an actively healthy growing plant and place these within the root zone of the new plant. Another method is to collect water that has passed through a pot containing a healthy, actively growing orchid of the same type, and use it to water the new plant/s.

Potting up container-grown orchids

When and how you repot, and how often, will vary considerably depending on the type of orchid you are growing and the conditions it is growing in.

Some orchids, including *Cymbidium* and many others, flower best when they are fairly rootbound. Annual potting up may, in this case, reduce the next season's flowering. Many plants, however, do their best when they are regularly repotted, as they grow, into larger containers with fresh potting mix. Repotting is normally carried out after the flowering period has finished.

A degree of root pruning is beneficial to some species but not all. Some orchids have very brittle roots that can be easily damaged if they are potted up, so you must be very careful when potting these.

Some orchids are easily disturbed by potting. In these cases potting or remounting is better left until it becomes really necessary.

In some situations, certain hardy types of orchids can grow rampant and flower so prolifically that they should be divided frequently, and the soil or media replenished in order to prevent their becoming starved of nutrients and deteriorating.

How you repot will depend on the species and the material to which roots are attached (bark chips or slabs or soil).

Choosing a container

Just about any container can be used for growing plants provided it will hold sufficient soil or potting mix for the plant to grow in, has suitable drainage, and does not contain or release any contaminants that may be harmful to plant growth. To get the best results, however, consider the following factors when choosing a container:

- Wider containers are more stable (less likely to tip over).
- Sufficient drainage holes are needed to allow excess water to drain away quickly. The holes should not be so big that potting mixes/soils can easily fall or wash out of the container. For orchids this may not be a problem, especially if coarse materials are used in the growing medium.
- The size of the container should be appropriate for the type of orchid you wish to grow. An orchid that will not grow very big will look out of place by itself in a large container, while a vigorous grower will soon outgrow a small one. Choose a large container to allow for such growth, or you will have to repot regularly.
- In deeper pots the weight of the potting mix/soil will compress the medium beneath and reduce air spaces in the mix. A more open mix should therefore be used for deeper pots.
- Plant roots tend to coil less in square pots than they do in round ones. Root coiling is also reduced if the base is more tapered.

Fertilisers

Orchid experts often disagree on feeding recommendations: one grower will say to feed regularly, and another very rarely. Different orchids do, of course, have different feeding requirements. If a plant looks weak and is putting on very little growth, it will usually benefit from a feed.

Generally, most orchids are not heavy feeders, and too much nutrient can burn the roots. They do, however, respond well to appropriate feeding. Slow release fertilisers, such as Osmocote or Nutricote, or a specially designed orchid food, are ideal, and plants often benefit from a weak solution of liquid fertiliser such as Aquasol or Phostrogen applied weekly during the growing season. Liquid seaweed fertilisers in weak doses can provide many of the trace elements, and organic fertilisers such as blood and bone, and bone meal, can also be readily used.

Fertilising is only needed when the plant is in active growth. When the plant is dormant, any fertiliser added will be mostly wasted (leached away) if the plant is subject to natural rainfall, or it can build up to dangerous levels if the plant is not being watered.

If an orchid potting mix is predominantly bark, then increased nitrogen application is recommended, so that the orchid need not compete with the bark for nitrogen as it breaks down over time.

Some orchid purists feed their orchids as though they are living naturally in the wild, using such materials as partly decayed leaf litter and small amounts of dead insects and dried bird droppings. Even old banana skins have been used.

Watering

If you understand the natural conditions your orchids are adapted to, then you can usually predict with a high degree of success how much and how often they will like to be watered.

Some species' natural habitat is swampland that is frequently or seasonally inundated. For these orchids (e.g. *Phaius tankervilliae*), mimicking the wet conditions at the right time of year is very important. Growers of orchids that come from cool mountainous districts, where winter enforces dormancy, would need to duplicate a cold winter, while orchids from dry regions like Western Australia will have a distinct hot dry summer, and will need to be watered accordingly. Epiphytic and lithophytic orchids generally require excellent drainage but fairly constant air moisture.

The amount of watering will depend on the species, the season, the natural rainfall, and the stage of growth of the plants you are watering.

As a general rule, all orchids in flower or actively growing will need to be watered regularly; however, excess watering will increase the likelihood of disease, cause root death, and possibly rotting of the entire plant. For plants that are adapted to rainforest conditions, high humidity may be very important; this could be provided by regular fine mist sprays. For orchids adapted to more arid conditions, less regular, but perhaps heavier, waterings may be appropriate.

Temperature

Just as the natural habitat of different orchids determines the amount of water each will tolerate, so it is with temperature. There is great variation in preferred temperatures between different types of orchids.

In general, the majority of the epiphytic species are found in sub-tropical and tropical climates, while the majority of terrestrial orchids are found in sub-tropical to temperate climates. These are generalisations, however, and there can be significant variations: for example, some tropical zone orchids may be found at high altitudes, where night temperatures can approach 0°C.

Many orchids require low temperatures to initiate flowering, so you may need to ensure that night temperatures are 5-10°C cooler than average day temperatures. For many orchids from warmer areas the optimum growing temperatures are in the range of 20-30°C, with active growth at temperatures above 15°C. For orchids adapted to cooler climates, growth may begin at temperatures as low as 5-10°C. Few orchids will thrive in temperatures over 30°C. To achieve optimum growth then, try to maintain temperatures that are neither too high nor too low.

Temperature is most readily controlled in a growing structure, such as a greenhouse or protected shadehouse, where mechanisms such as heaters, evaporative coolers, misting systems, exhaust fans and adjustable vents can be used, or the floor of the growing structure can be dampened down.

On a small scale, positions that offer a little more warmth than general surrounding conditions may provide sufficient protection. You could simply place your plants under a tree to minimise the risk of frost exposure, under the eaves of a house (be careful to ensure adequate watering), or perhaps on a protected window sill (inside or outside) as long as the plants are not exposed to too much light or direct sunlight.

Ventilation

Ventilation not only helps to control temperatures and humidity in the orchids' growing areas, but also ensures adequate exchange of air so that there is enough carbon dioxide for optimum growth. Carbon dioxide is essential in the process of photosynthesis, being one of the raw materials converted into the carbohydrates necessary for plant growth (e.g. stored energy).

Many orchids open their stomata (pores in their leaves) just after sunrise to allow the movement of air (including carbon dioxide) into the leaves. The pores close again just after sunset, so good air movement is essential during the day, particularly around daybreak. However, some orchids, such as many tropical epiphytes, need to conserve the moisture that would be lost to the atmosphere through the stomata when they are open, so during the day they keep their stomata closed. As temperatures drop after dark, and water loss is not as much of a problem, they open their stomata to allow carbon dioxide to pass into the leaf to be stored. For this type of plant ventilation is therefore most important at night. In cooler areas where heating may be required, especially during winter, ventilation could be very expensive.

Orchids as indoor plants

Some orchids can be grown for a period inside a house, but many of the conditions that are comfortable for people are not ideal for orchids.

Growing plants in containers is the most common way of using plants indoors, and there are four major factors that need to be considered. These are:

- Temperature: sudden changes are usually the biggest problem. These can be caused by heaters/air conditioners going on and off, doors opening and closing, and/or cooking appliances operating in the kitchen.
- Light: too bright a light (e.g. near a window) or too dull can be equally detrimental. Lights being turned on and off, or being used for extensive periods, can affect plants' physiological response (photoperiodism). Dust on leaves can block up leaf pores (stomata) and also reduce the amount of light reaching the leaf itself.
- Moisture: low humidity/dry air (particularly when heaters are being used) will affect the plants' wellbeing. And remember there is no natural rainfall to keep foliage moist (or to wash off dust).
- Gases/ventilation: many orchids need good ventilation to reduce the likelihood of disease, or they might prefer high humidity. They might need the delicate balance of gases found in fresh air, which can be difficult to provide indoors.

Controlling pests and diseases

If you maintain the right levels of temperature, humidity, light and water you will have fewer problems with pests and diseases. A healthy plant is more likely to resist attack, and will recover more readily if it is attacked. Check any plants carefully before you buy them for signs of pests and/or disease. Bringing even one infected plant home could soon result in the rapid spread of the problem/s to your other plants, and not just your orchids.

When numbers of plants of the one species or group are grown in a confined area, such as a greenhouse, pests and disease can spread rapidly.

Inspect your plants regularly so that you can detect and control any problems as early as possible. This will minimise the risk of their spreading, as well as the need for you to use expensive, and perhaps dangerous, control methods. Remove any dead or diseased plants, or quarantine those that are diseased so that you can use control methods to eradicate the pest and/or the disease.

Good hygiene is extremely important. Thoroughly clean tools and equipment (e.g. secateurs, pots) prior to use. Ideally, dip cutting tools in disinfectant between use on different plants. Keeping plants up off the ground on benches, or in baskets, etc., will minimise the spread of pests and diseases from the ground. Soil harbours many of these, so minimise contact between your plants and soil to reduce the risk of infection. Watering cans, hoses and nozzles should be stored off the ground as disease spores can easily be spread when watering if, for example, your hose nozzle has been sitting in a stagnant pool.

If you are going to try a new chemical to control pests and diseases on your plants, it is best to trial spray a few before using it extensively. This ensures that if the spray causes damage (known as phytotoxicity) then the minimum number of plants will suffer.

PESTS

Chewing insects: these commonly attack orchids and include weevils, Cattleya fly, cockroaches, palmetto bugs, springtails and grasshoppers. The orchid beetle (dendrobium beetle) can cause major problems by larvae tunnelling through the canes. Carbaryl-based sprays or dusts are effective against most chewing insects. You can also remove small infestations very effectively by hand.

Sucking insects: those that may attack your orchids are thrips, mealy bugs, aphids, and red spider mite. Malathion is one of the most widely used insecticides for controlling pests like these. Systemic insecticides are useful in dealing with sucking insects.

Scale: these are also sucking insects, and may be controlled by rubbing the plants gently with a soft brush and plenty of soapy water. Use Confidor for a heavy infestation.

Snails and slugs: watch your orchids carefully for these. If you use snail baits, ensure that children and animals can't get at them. Replace them regularly for maximum effectiveness. Alternative non-chemical controls, such as placing saucers of stale beer around to attract and then drown the snails, have proven relatively successful. Once again, provide regular supplies.

DISEASES

In general, diseases pose more of a risk to your orchids than do pests. Fungal and bacterial diseases thrive in the warm temperatures and high humidity preferred by many orchids. These diseases can spread rapidly and cause major damage or death to your plants if you do not control them.
Some of the more common diseases that affect orchids include:

Water moulds (*Pythium* and *Phytophthora*): these are also known as damping off diseases. They are found in damp growing media and poorly ventilated conditions. They can rapidly spread, damaging roots, stems and leaves of many plants besides orchids. Often before you realise it, serious damage is done, particularly to roots. Young seedlings in community pots are most at risk.

The best method of control is prevention. Ensure good hygiene, good drainage in growing media, and good ventilation around your plants. Chemical control can be achieved by drenching the growing media with the systemic fungicide, Fongarid.

Leaf spots: these can be caused by a number of different fungi and bacteria. The symptoms of leaf spots can usually be seen early on in the spread of the disease, so controls can be quickly applied. Leaf spots caused by fungi can be treated with a variety of fungicides, including copper-based sprays (e.g. Copper oxychloride, Kocide), and Mancozeb. Effectiveness of these sprays will vary according to which fungus is causing the problem, and as resistance can develop within some fungi it may be necessary to alternate the chemicals you use for the most effective control. Cutting off and burning infected parts can also help reduce the risk of leaf spots spreading, as can reducing humidity and increasing ventilation. Bacterial leaf spots cannot be controlled by fungicides (some degree of trial and error may be necessary here), and diseased plant parts may need to be cut off, or the plants removed and destroyed.

Powdery mildew: this condition normally affects the leaves or flowers of orchids. It is most prevalent in warm or humid conditions, particularly if the growing medium is dry. It shows as white or grey-white fur or patches. It spreads quickly causing death to parts of or the whole plant. It can be controlled by removing and burning infected parts. Spray with a copper-based fungicide (e.g. Kocide), Dinocap or wettable sulphur (in cool conditions only), or Mancozeb.

Flower spotting: this group of diseases also spreads rapidly in high humidity and poor ventilation. Older flowers are most commonly attacked. Remove these, lower the humidity, and increase ventilation. Spraying with a fungicide will often damage younger flowers, but may be necessary if the problem is extensive.

Use fungicides with care. For those growers who encourage development of mycorrhiza, fungicides may in fact be detrimental.

VIRUSES

There is no successful treatment at present for viral infections of orchids, so the only control measure is to destroy and burn infected plants. It is often difficult to tell when a plant is infected by a virus as several diseases can produce the same symptoms. Signs can include severe colour breaks in the flowers, and/or irregular yellow areas along the leaves, which later turn black.

If you suspect your plants are infected, it is best to act promptly by destroying them. Since the virus lives in the sap of the plant all secateurs and knives that you use in the process should be dipped in methylated spirits and flamed before cutting another plant. Also wash your hands thoroughly before handling other plants.

It is important that you obtain any new plants from reputable suppliers to minimise the risk of bringing infected plants home.

Propagating orchids

Orchids can all be propagated by seed. This is usually done in aseptic (sterilised) flasks, using techniques similar to those applied to tissue culture. Most can also be grown successfully by tissue culture.

Some orchids can be grown by other techniques, for example, *Cymbidium* can be grown from back bulbs (pseudobulbs); *Epidendrum* (e.g. crucifix orchids) can be grown from stem cuttings; many (e.g. *Dendrobium*) can be grown by division of offsets or separation; well-developed plants of terrestrial orchids (such as *Paphiopedilum*) can be divided just before active growth begins.

Propagation methods

SEXUAL OR ASEXUAL PROPAGATION

Sexual propagation produces progeny where each of two parents contributes genetic material. Seed propagation is the most common sexual method of propagation. The plants produced will be variable in characteristics. Sexual methods are used for breeding new varieties, or, in the case of rare orchids, for maintaining biodiversity – ensuring a wider gene pool.

Asexual propagation produces progeny from only one parent. The plants produced are genetically the same as the parent. This is sometimes called cloning. Asexual methods are used when you want to produce new plants whose characteristics are identical (e.g. flower size and colour) to those of the parent.

SYMPODIAL EPIPHYTES

This group includes *Cattleya*, *Cymbidium* and *Odontoglossum* orchids.

When the plant is overgrown in the pot, the rhizome attached to the pseudobulb can be partly cut and then left until new growth begins on it, or completely severed and the pseudobulb immediately planted separate from the rest of the plant. With *Cattleya*, each new plant should have three or more pseudobulbs. With *Cymbidium*, one pseudobulb is sufficient for a new plant, but it may take a few years to flower.

MONOPODIAL EPIPHYTES

Orchids such as *Vanda* develop white aerial roots on the stems as they grow upwards. When the stems have developed a good crop of these aerial roots, sections of stem can then be taken as stem cuttings. Roots can be left on such cuttings.

AERIAL OFFSETS

Orchids such as *Dendrobium* produce plantlets (keikis) at the end of existing pseudobulbs. These may be removed and potted up individually or left on the plant to grow and flower. If they are removed, it is best to wait until they are about 15 cm long to ensure a good success rate. Then sever them from the parent plant and attach them to the appropriate substrate (e.g. cork tile).

PROPAGATION BY SEED

It can be quite difficult to germinate orchid seeds, and to grow them on to produce seedlings to a transplantable size. It is usually best to leave this to the experts. Specialist equipment and knowledge are needed, and the subject is beyond the scope of this book. There are many orchid growers who specialise in selling young seedlings to orchid enthusiasts. These are often sold as flasks containing a few too many seedlings (e.g. 30 or so) and these can be removed from the flask and carefully potted up. These seedlings generally have been raised from seed produced from carefully pollinated flowers. Parents with the desired characteristics are chosen, with the hope that some or all of these will be passed on to their progeny. Often the growers who sell you the flask will arrange to buy back any superior plants, or plants with unusual characteristics, that you have raised from the seedlings they supplied to you.

Some specialist growers will also produce (for a fee) seedlings from seed that you supply to them. This can be an ideal way to start producing your own new varieties of orchids, without having to, at least initially, obtain the equipment and expertise required to germinate the seed. It is best to ask around, and find out what the specialists would charge you, and what conditions they might apply.

You can always try for 'pot luck' results by collecting seed from a plant without knowing which other plant supplied the pollen. Alternatively, you can choose the plants you wish to use as parents, and actually collect pollen from one and use it to pollinate the other.

HARVESTING ORCHID SEED

As the seed pods mature they change colour, usually yellowing. You must watch the plants carefully, and when they start to show signs of splitting along the placenta, and not before, harvest the seed into a polythene or paper bag. From one plant you may have as many as a million or so viable seeds, or as few as a dozen. (There can be nearly 3 million seeds in one pod of a *Cymbidium tracyanum*.)

Greenhouse and shadehouse structures

It is always easier and more economical to grow orchids that share a liking for your own natural environment. However, many growers wish to grow those that would not normally thrive outdoors in their area. The further a specific orchid plant is removed from its natural habitat, the more likely you will need an artificial structure to keep it alive and well. For example, someone in London or Melbourne wanting to grow *Phalaenopsis* will require a glasshouse or similar structure with heating. Someone in Cairns or California may need a shadehouse and cooling equipment to successfully grow species that come from temperate zones.

Greenhouses, shadehouses, cold frames and cloches are all structures used to protect plants from inhospitable environments and to provide better growing conditions.

A **greenhouse** is a building with a roof (and often sides) made from glass, plastic or some other material that will allow light and warmth to enter during the day, thus creating enhanced conditions for plant growth. Ideally a greenhouse will retain overnight some of the warmth gathered during the day.

A **shadehouse** is a partly or fully enclosed structure with a roof (and sometimes sides) made from a material that filters light entering the area, to provide more suitable (lower) light intensities for plants growing there.

A **cold frame** is a small enclosed structure with a lift-up or lift-off roof. It is essentially a small glasshouse, and performs a similar job, but you cannot walk inside. A cold frame can be useful for propagating plants, or for protecting them in limited numbers.

A **cloche** is a small plastic or glass cover (perhaps only 30 cm tall) which can be placed over plants when they are young and susceptible to frosts, then removed later in the season as the plants begin to establish and there is no further danger from frost.

Why use a protective structure?

The main reason for using a greenhouse, shadehouse or some similar structure is to provide a better environment for your plants.

Greenhouses can:

- create and maintain a higher temperature than the outside environment;
- protect plants from frost;
- create a more humid environment than that outside;
- create an environment with a different balance of gases from that found in the fresh air outside;
- provide some degree of protection from wind, hail and pests.

Shadehouses can:

- create a darker environment suitable for plants that prefer less intense light;
- remove the danger of sunburn for sensitive plants;
- protect from frosts;
- provide a shady, protected environment for human use;
- provide a more humid environment from that outside.

All too often, however, people put plants in such structures just because they have them, when the plants might well have been better off left outside.

Remember:

- some varieties of orchids prefer cooler temperatures than you will find in greenhouses;
- most orchids that prefer a greenhouse environment will benefit from a spell outside for at least part of the year;
- orchids that prefer a shadehouse in the intense summer sun may require a position with more light during winter.

Greenhouses

There are many different types of greenhouses available today: each has its advantages and disadvantages. Generally speaking, the old adage applies: 'You get what you pay for.' The cheaper greenhouses generally don't do as good a job, and they are less permanent. The expensive greenhouses can last a lifetime and will, in many respects, do a better job. The initial cost, however, may be a deterrent.

CONSTRUCTION

Shortwall: the transparent material covers the roof and only part of each of the sides. The rest is covered with non-transparent material such as timber or brick.

Longwall: the transparent material covers each entire wall and all of the roof.

Tunnel: the framework is made from half-circle metal hoops arranged in a row to form a tunnel shape. Transparent material is laid over this framework (PVC film or more solid plastics are most commonly used).

Lean-to: this is a structure attached to the side of another building (e.g. your house). The other building provides one side-wall for the greenhouse.

FRAMING MATERIALS

Metal: aluminium frames are popular because they resist rusting. Galvanised iron or steel are also used, though over time corrosion can become a problem. While glass works well with metal, PVC film and other plastics can deteriorate if they are in direct contact with metal. For example, metal will get very hot in summer, and the sections of PVC film touching it will crack or tear much sooner than those parts not in contact.

Timber: timber does not heat up like metal; however, it may rot, particularly in the humid environment of a greenhouse. Some treated timbers will last for many years, but it is important to check that the materials used in treating the wood are non-toxic to plants. Pests such as mealybugs and cockroaches may also breed in timber.

COVERING/CLADDING MATERIALS

When choosing covering materials consider the following properties:

- insulation – ability to hold heat in;
- light transmission – how much of the light reaching the greenhouse will travel through the covering to the plants? Covering materials are best if they are clear, not coloured. Green fibreglass, which has been popular with many home gardeners in the past, actually does not promote good plant growth or flowers;
- cost – some materials are far more expensive initially;
- lifespan – how long it will be before the material needs to be replaced;
- flexibility – more flexible materials are easier to build with;
- durability – how much wear and tear can they withstand?

Glass:

- is expensive;
- is rigid, so it is only suited to straight-walled or roofed greenhouses;
- is not easily cut to size or shape;
- shatters if hit solidly, leaving jagged fragments;
- generally is used in small sections so it can be easily replaced, but heat losses can be high if sections are not butted up to each other carefully;
- allows good light passage;
- is long-lived if looked after.

PVC film:

- is cheap;
- is not long-lived, usually only 2-3 years unless it contains inhibitors against UV light which breaks the plastic down, in which case it may last five years;
- is easily cut to size or shape;
- allows good light passage;
- is flexible, so is good for curved surfaces;
- is easily damaged;
- comes in large rolls so it is easily applied, and minimises gaps so heat losses are reduced.

Reinforced PVC film:

- is the same as PVC film, but with woven thread embedded in the plastic to provide reinforcement; this improves its strength and durability;
- allows slightly less light transmission than PVC film, which at times can be an advantage;
- is more expensive than other PVC films.

Polyflute/Corflute:

- has a medium life span (seven years or more);
- is moderately expensive;
- is easily cut to size or shape;
- is semi-rigid so it can be used on gentle curves;
- comes in large sheets or rolls so it is easily attached;
- is double-layered which cuts down on heat loss;
- is slightly opaque so light passage is not as good as glass or polythene;
- will withstand some impact, so it won't shatter or tear easily, and can be repaired in some cases.

Rigid plastic sheeting (e.g. Polycarbonate):

- has a medium life span;
- is semi-rigid and only suited to easy curves;
- is available in a variety of colours – clear ones give good light passage, but not as good as glass or PVC film;
- is fairly expensive;
- is usually available in corrugated or Greca profiles; not being flat, heat loss can be a problem;
- is fairly easy to cut;
- will withstand some impact – won't shatter or tear easily;
- is available in large sheets, which easily overlap.

PROBLEMS WITH GREENHOUSES

The following are some of the most common problems experienced with growing plants in greenhouses. Watch out for:

- overheating – on a hot day, the greenhouse temperature can rise very quickly and overheat plants before you realise it;
- frost damage – a severe frost will penetrate the sides and roof of even the best built greenhouses. If the house isn't heated, keep your most tender plants in the centre away from the walls;
- diseases and pests that can breed and spread faster in the greenhouse environment than outside. Problems need to be watched for closely and treated quickly;
- plants drying out – the extra warmth in a greenhouse means that plants in pots dry out faster and need watering more often.

Shadehouses

Shadehouses are used to protect plants from hot sun, wind or excessively bright light. They are also useful for conditioning plants to the outside environment after they have been protected in a greenhouse : a tender plant is often taken from a greenhouse to a shadehouse for a period to allow it to adapt to less ideal conditions, before being put outside. Shadehouses provide an ideal growing environment for many types of orchids and ferns in most parts of Australia.

MATERIALS

Framing materials are the same as for greenhouses. Covering materials, however, are different. Their function is to reduce light transmission while allowing the free passage of gases, and the free or partially restricted passage of rainfall.

The most commonly used materials are tea tree brush, wooden slats or shadecloth. The latter material can be obtained in various grades that represent different levels of light transmission. For example, a 50% shadecloth reduces light transmission by 50%. Your choice will depend on your plants' individual needs.

Greenhouse or shadehouse?

When deciding on which type of structure would best protect your orchids, it is important to keep a few simple points in mind. These include:

- plant growth requirements – do you really need a glasshouse or will a shadehouse be adequate?
- space – how much space do you have available to set up your structure; how much space do you need for the number of orchids you wish to grow?
- cost – how much are you prepared to spend?
- product availability – is it easy to get; are spares, etc. easy to obtain?
- ease of construction – do you have the necessary expertise to build one of these structures; is a kit form the best option; or would you pay someone else to set it up?
- lifespan – is this just a whim or a deep abiding interest; will you be at the same location for a long time; how much effort are you prepared to spend on repairs and maintenance?
- local by-laws – are there any regulations that govern use of such structures in your area, for example, size limitations?

The staff of reputable greenhouse suppliers are generally well-informed and can recommend the best greenhouse for each grower's requirements. If in doubt, ask around among other orchid enthusiasts for advice on suppliers of greenhouses and associated equipment.

Temperature control in greenhouses

Temperature can be controlled in a greenhouse in several ways:

- The sun will warm the greenhouse during the day. This effect varies according to the time of year, time of day and the weather conditions that day. The way the greenhouse is built and the materials used in construction will also influence the house's ability to catch heat from the sun, and hold that heat.

- Heaters can be used to add to the heat in a house. The heater must be able to replace heat at the same rate at which it is being lost to the outside.
- Vents and doors can be opened to let cool air into the greenhouse, or closed to stop warm air from escaping.
- Shade cloth can be drawn over the house to stop the warm sun penetrating. Greenhouse paints or whitewash can be applied in spring for the same effect. The type of paint used is normally one that will last the summer, but wash off with weathering to allow warming light to penetrate in winter.
- Coolers (e.g. air blowers, evaporative coolers) can be used to lower the temperature.
- Watering, misting or fogging systems will be effective in lowering temperatures.
- Exhaust fans can be used to decrease the temperature.
- Water storage in tanks or drums under the floor or the benches of a glasshouse can act as a buffer to temperature fluctuations by absorbing heat during the day, and releasing it slowly at night.
- Double glazing of greenhouses, or adding plastic liners, can be very effective in minimising heat loss. The layer of air trapped between the layers of glass, or between the glass and the plastic liner, acts as an insulator. The plastic layer can be removed in summer, when conditions are warmer.

HEAT LOSS THROUGH COVERING MATERIALS

An important consideration in temperature control is the heat lost through the walls and the roof of the house. Each type of covering material (e.g. glass, plastic, etc.) differs in its capacity to retain heat. Heat is normally measured in British Thermal Units (BTUs). The table below shows the respective qualities of different materials.

Covering material	*Heat loss* (BTU/sq.ft/hr)
Glass (6 mm thick)	1.13
Double layer glass	0.65
Fibreglass reinforced plastic	1.0
Rigid plastic sheet (3 mm thick) (e.g. polycarbonate)	1.0
Polythene film	1.15
Polythene film (double layer)	0.70

(Table from *Greenhouse Operation*, Nelson, Prentice Hall)

HEATERS

There are several types of heaters that are commonly used in domestic and small commercial greenhouses. The advantages of each of these heaters depends on the initial cost, the possible lifespan and, particularly, the running cost of fuels. These will vary from area to area. The main types of heaters used are:

- Unit heaters burn fuels such as oil or gas, and the resultant heat rises through thin metal pipes or tubes. A fan blows air through these pipes or tubes and the air is heated. This gives a more even heat spread than convection heaters.

- Convection heaters differ from unit heaters in that they do not have a heat exchanger such as the pipe or tube system, but create heat from the direct combustion of fuels. Hot fumes pass out through an exhaust pipe. The pipe needs to be long enough to prevent dangerously hot air from coming in contact with plants.

- Electric heaters that consist generally of a heating element and a fan that blows air across the element and into the glasshouse can be very cheap to run if you happen to have cheap electricity. Costs can be as low as two cents per hour (for a 2000 watt heater) in some parts of Australia, but up to 15 cents per hour in others. Take care that moisture (e.g. from misting systems) doesn't cause problems with the heater and any wiring.

- Radiant heaters, such as low energy infra-red heaters, have become popular in the US. They are considered to be very cheap to operate.

- Solar heaters are generally very economical to run; however, depending on your location, these may not viable. While they may be the best option in areas of high solar radiation, in low solar areas they may be ineffective.

- Heat can also be obtained from composting organic matter such as fresh animal manures or sawdust. These materials can be spread as a layer on a section of the floor of the greenhouse, and as they compost they release a lot of heat. However, this heat source is irregular and generally only of use for a few months. It may be a cheap option if a ready supply of such materials is available, particularly for small structures such as cold frames. It is important that plants are not placed directly on such materials, unless you are experienced with their use, as they can generate quite high temperatures at times. Diseases may possibly spread with this type of heating procedure.

Table of requirements of selected orchid genera

Genera	*Minimum temperature (Celsius)*	*Habit*	*Where to grow*	*Shade requirements*
Ascocentrum	10-15	Epiphytic	Pots	Heavy-medium
Brassavola	15	Epiphytic	Pots	Essential
Brassia	15	Epiphytic	Pots	Essential in summer
Bulbophyllum	18	Epiphytic	Pots or wood slabs	Medium
Cattleya	12	Epiphytic	Pots	Mild-medium
Coelogyne	10	Epiphytic	Pots and baskets	Mild-medium
Cymbidium	7 or lower	Epiphytic or terrestrial	Pots	Medium
Dendrobium	some 10, others lower	Mainly epiphytic	Wood/fern slabs, pots or baskets	Light-medium shade in summer
Epidendrum	some 10, others lower	Epiphytic	Pots, beds or baskets	Light medium
Laelia	10	Epiphytic	Pots	Mild-medium
Masdavillea	10	Epiphytic	Pots	Mild
Odontoglossum	15	Epiphytic	Pots	Mild
Oncidium	15	Epiphytic	Pots or slabs	Mild
Paphiopedilum	13	Terrestrial	Pots	Medium to heavy
Phalaenopsis	18	Epiphytic	Pots or baskets	70-80%
Pleione	10 or lower	Epiphytic or terrestrial	Pots	Mild-medium
Vanda	12-20	Epiphytes	Usually slabs occasionally pots	Essential in summer
Zygopetalum	12-15	Epiphytes	Pots, baskets or slabs	Mild

A~Z of Easy Orchids

What's in a name?

Orchids are a very large and diverse range of plants. As a result, naming a genus is not always as straightforward as it could be. There are literally hundreds of new cultivars and two or three new genera (intergeneric) registered every month. Classification is an evolving science and changes occur continually. The following information may help to explain why you have difficulty in locating a particular orchid.

Some plants, which are actually hybrids, have been given an intergeneric name that is used as the genus. Others have been given one name which is later changed to another, or the plant is reclassified. For instance, plants in the genus *Rhyncholaelia* were once considered to be of the genus *Brassavola*. Some sources now class them separately, as we have in this book, while some have chosen to keep them as *Brassavola*. Most newer texts will use the two separate names, or indicate that they are sometimes considered synonymous. However, this is not always the case, especially in older texts.

Cross pollination of orchids, to create a new and unique plant, occurs regularly. In some instances, the resulting hybrid is referred to as a new genus. These names are actually intergeneric names. For example, Zygowarrea is the genus name for a cross of *Warrea lindley* × *Zygopetalum hooker* (Zygo + Warrea). All other plants then hybridised from *Zygowarrea* will likely be given the intergeneric genus name of *Zygowarrea*. Intergeneric names can also be given in honour of a particular person; this usually occurs when several plants have been crossed to breed the plant. For instance, the intergeneric name *Alangreatwoodara* is in honour of plant breeder Alan Greatwood, with the original plant in the 'genus' being a cross of three orchids.

To add to the confusion, all genus and intergeneric names are given an abbreviation. So you may see a plant identified as *Ascda*.'Park Yon Kyoung'. In this instance, the full stop indicates an abbreviation. However, if that full stop does not appear, as is often the case, there is no indication that Ascda is the accepted abbreviation for the genus *Ascocenda*.

We have covered a great range of orchids in this book, but due to the constant changes as detailed above, it is nearly impossible to include every genus, intergeneric name and cultivar in one publication. However, the knowledge of how the names evolve, and a little detective work. can help you to find out about your orchids.

Orchid name conventions

The first name (referred to as the *Genus*) begins with a capital letter and is written in italics.

The second name is usually the *species* if it is written with a small letter, and is also in italics.

Some second names that start with a capital letter are also species names.

Most orchid names, however, have only genus and cultivar name: genus is always in italics, cultivar is not. For example, *Phalaenopsis* Orchid World

Some will have genus, species and cultivar names. For example, *Thelymitra nuda* 'Tall White'.

AERIDES

(Abbreviation – Aersa.)

Aerides are related to *Vanda* and *Phalaenopsis*. The genus consists of 40-60 species of epiphytes, coming mainly from tropical Asia and South East Asia, with some from the South West Pacific.

The pendulous flowers appear in lateral, sometimes branching, racemes and are often fragrant, and waxy in texture. Most are monopodial (i.e. having single stems) and the stems produce thick roots. Foliage can vary, from strap-like to narrow and long, and rounded.

Some cultivars are relatively tall, growing to well over 1 m, while others rarely reach more than 0.5 m.

Culture

Aerides are ideally suited to a rainforest environment. Their culture is very similar to *Vanda*, and they are best grown attached to a fibrous backing such as a tree fern, or some moss on a board, provided it isn't too acidic. They also grow well in an open basket. Growing them in a pot on a bench is more difficult. Repot or remount infrequently, as it is best not to disturb the brittle roots.

Aerides grow best in bright light and require a warm greenhouse in temperate climates. Most species prefer climates with temperatures from 15-30°C, and humidity in excess of 50%. Some will tolerate cooler climates (e.g. *A. multiflora* and *A. vandarum*).

As the lower leaves get older, they may drop off, exposing sections of stem which will grow roots. You can propagate plants by removing such a section from a branching plant in spring. Be sure to take some healthy roots.

Cultivars

A. crassifolium (syn. *A. crassifolia*) produces fragrant reddish-purple flowers which have a greenish tip to the lip, and leaves to 20 cm long. It is sometimes called 'King of Aerides'.

A. crispa (syn. *A. crispum*) develops scented flowers with rose-coloured markings and a 3-lobed and fringed lip that is white to purplish. There are several named varieties, some growing to 1.5 m tall.

A. falcata var. *Houlletiana* (syn. *A. houlletiana*) produces brownish-yellow sepals and petals with a slightly fringed cream or white lip displaying a magenta patch.

A. falcatum (syn. *A. falcata*) can grow up to 1 m tall, and differs from *A. houlletiana* (see below) in that the lip is not fringed and the flower colour can be a little different.

A. houlletiana produces cream-yellow flowers with a pink lip which is fringed or lightly serrated.

A. japonica (syn. *A. japonicum*) is a low-growing orchid which produces white to greenish-white flowers with red to purplish markings.

A. Lawrenciae produces predominantly cream or white flowers with red to purplish markings, and stems to 1 m.

A. multiflorum (syn. *A. multiflora*) prefers even moisture all year and good sunlight in order to produce white and purple flowers to 2.5 cm across in summer.

A. odoratum (syn. *A. odorata, A. suavissima*) develops spicy fragrant white flowers with purple blotches to 2 cm across, and foliage 1.8 m long .

Hybrids

Aerides have been interbred with various related genera, such as *Phalaenopsis*, to produce hybrids.

ARACHNIS (SCORPION ORCHID)

(Abbreviation – Arach.)

This genus contains seven species, which are found naturally in Thailand and China. They are epiphytic orchids, with a stem that will wrap around, and occasionally climb, trees. Flowers are typically yellow or pink with purplish-brown stripes or spots, and can occur all year round. The flower spikes can carry few flowers, or many.

Certain species from this genus are sometimes known as *Vanda*, or *Esmeralda*.

Culture

These orchids prefer warm, humid conditions and need full sun to bloom. As with *Aranda*, they are best suited to a greenhouse in most locations. Plants can be propagated by separation.

Cultivars

A. Cathcartii (syn. *Esmeralda Cathcartii*) has a stem that can grow up to 2 m long, and leaves up to 15 cm. Flowers are yellow with brownish-red stripes, around 9 cm wide, and there are 3-5 on each spike. The lip is white with red and yellow markings.

A. flos-aeris (the Spider Orchid) is a large plant to 1.5 m, with many greenish-yellow, purple-spotted flowers on each spike.

A. Hookerana produces cream flowers with purple stripes and/or spots, and stems to 70 cm long.

A. Lowii can grow stems up to 2 m, with very large leaves (80 cm long), and produces orange flower with purple-red spots.

Hybrids

There are hybrids both within this genus and with other closely related genera.

A. Maingayi is a hybrid of *A. flos-aeris* with *A. Hookerana*. It is similar to *A. flos-aeris*, but with smaller flowers, predominantly pink marked with pink or purple spots.

Aranda are hybrids of *Arachnis hookeriana* with *Vanda*.

They are easy to grow, but need consistent heat, humidity and light to produce flowers. *Aranda* Wong Bee Yeok produces strong purple flowers.

ARANDA (see *Arachnis* above)

Masdevallia
Veitchiana 'Sol'

PHOTO: GARY YONG GEE

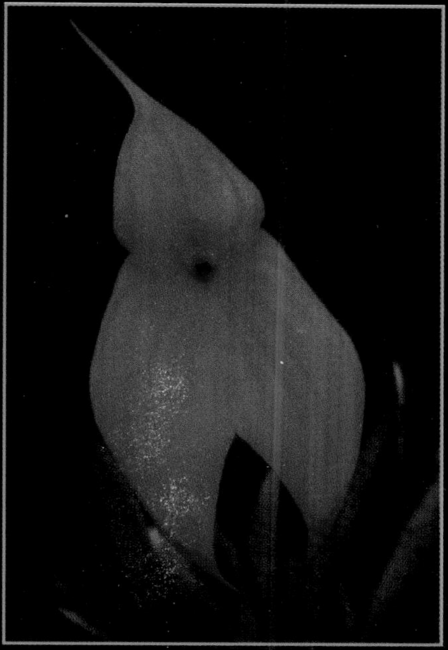

Oncidium Golden Shower

Ascocenda Park Yon Kyoung

. *Phaius flavus* PHOTO: GARY YONG GEE

Bulbophyllum graveolens (syn. *Cirrhopetalum graveolens*) PHOTO: GARY YONG GEE

Dendrobium formosum

Paphiopedilum St. Swithin 'Hannah' PHOTO: GARY YONG GEE

Phalaenopsis Ho's Queen Brother

Encyclia cordigera
PHOTO: GARY YONG GEE

Dendrobium Bangkok Fancy

Sarcochilus Hartmannii

Miltonia Jean Carlson 'Desire'

Laelia purpurata PHOTO: GARY YONG GEE

ARUNDINA (BAMBOO ORCHIDS)

These terrestrials occur naturally in sunny places from the Himalayas and China to South East Asia and the Pacific, from sea level to altitudes of around 1000 m. They are often found growing in tall grass near a watercourse. The reed-like stems with linear leaves give the plants a bamboo-like appearance.

The terminal flowers are generally pale pinkish to purple in colour.

Culture

These orchids must have a bright light, but direct hot sun can burn the leaves, which will turn yellow and drop. Keep the plants moist all year while ensuring they have excellent drainage. A reasonable potting medium is three parts organic loam to one part organic material such as compost or peat moss. They respond to organic or slow-release artificial fertilisers.

Arundina require temperatures that are never below 18° and rarely above 30°C. They need up to 90% shade over summer in warmer parts of Australia if temperatures ever go above 30°C. In winter reduce shade to 70%.

They will grow in pots, but generally do better in the ground, undisturbed.

Propagate by dividing mature plants; avoid disturbing young ones.

Cultivars

A. bambusifolia (syn *A. graminifolia*) can grow to 2 m tall, and exhibit large flowers of variable markings. An established clump under good conditions can produce 60 or more flower spikes each year. This species probably encompasses a large number of naturally occurring hybrids, so classification has been confused, often being split into several genera.

A. chinensis has light green foliage to 1.2 m tall, and flowers with pale mauve petals and a darker purplish lip with yellow markings in the throat.

A. densa flowers in summer, with fragrant rose to crimson blossoms.

Arundina chinensis

ASCOCENDA (see *Ascocentrum* below)

(Abbreviation – Ascda)

ASCOCENTRUM (syn. *Saccolabium*)

(Abbreviation – Asctm.)

Related to *Vanda*, the *Ascocentrum* genus is made up of five species of small epiphytes. They are indigenous to Asia and South East Asia, and are usually found in highlands above 1500 m.

The plant produces several flowers densely arranged on short spikes, with petals and sepals that are similar, and a spurred lip. Flower colours range from white to yellow or reddish tones. Leaves are short, linear and relatively numerous.

Culture

Pot in an open coarse medium and feed by spraying liquid fertiliser onto the potting material or applying slow release fertiliser when root growth is active. The plants will grow well in an open slat basket. If using a plastic pot, split the sides to increase drainage.

Most *Ascocentrum* need a minimum temperature of 12°C and humidity of 50% or more. The ideal climate would normally be considered tropical to sub-tropical with minimal shade. They prefer less shade than most other epiphytic orchids, but direct sun can burn them.

Propagate by division of mature plants.

Cultivars

A. ampullaceum has short stems and thick leaves. It produces large numbers of carmine-rose flowers each with a spurred lip.

A. curvifolium has thick leaves and orange to yellow flowers.

A. garayi has plump peach-pink flowers.

A. Henersonianum produces carmine flowers with a white lip above the fleshy leaves.

A. miniatum is a short plant with upright stems and bright red to orange or yellowish flowers in spring to early summer. Flower colour is best if the plant is kept in very bright light but not direct sunlight.

A. pumilum is a small plant no taller than 6 cm, with a flower spike carrying 2-10 pinkish flowers.

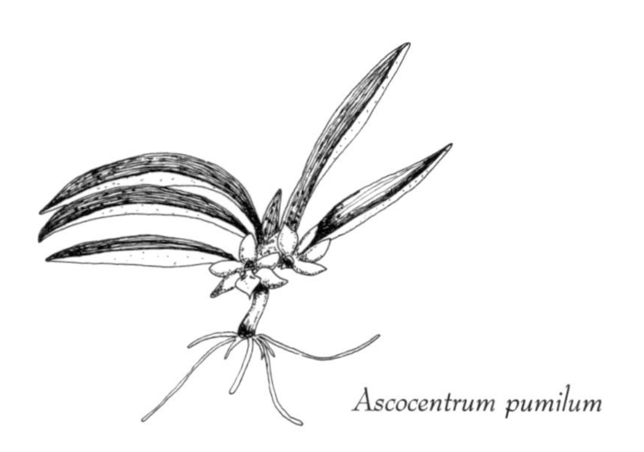

Ascocentrum pumilum

Hybrids

Ascocenda is an intergeneric cross between *Ascocentrum* and *Vanda*, it is a smaller and often more colourful plant than Vanda. See Vanda for cultural information.

Ascda. Pranam produces orange flowers.

Ascda. Park Yon Kyoung develops red-orange to yellow flowers.

Ascda. Thonglor x*V. coerulea* has a lavender mosaic pattern.

AULIZA (see *Epidendrum*)

BLETIA

There are between 25 and 50 species (note that reputable authorities are in conflict) of these normally terrestrial orchids, all native to tropical America. In rare instances, some can be epiphytic.

Bletia is related to *Calanthe*, but the lip has a slightly different structure. Flowers are generally brightly coloured, but not big and occur in small or large numbers. Most *Bletia* are summer flowering. Leaves are long and narrow, and can be grass-like. Some species can grow stems to around 1 m long.

Culture

A good potting medium is 1 part loam, 1 part well-rotted compost or leaf mould and 1 part chunky bark or charcoal. Repot as soon as new growth appears.

Water freely when the plant is putting on growth but give very little water when it is dormant (which can be up to four months or more).

Avoid temperatures below 15°C.

Propagate by division after flowering.

Cultivars

B. catenulata produces large pink, blood-red or purple flowers, each to 4 cm across, during the warmer months. It is native to Ecuador, Peru, Bolivia and Brazil.

B. patula can grow stems to 70 cm or more. It can produce pink or magenta flowers all year, and is native to the West Indies.

B. purpurea (syn. *B. alata*) is a deciduous terrestrial orchid (rarely epiphytic) with pink to rose-purple flowers borne on a raceme up to 50 cm long. Flower size and colour may vary. Stems grow to 1.5 m long. It is native to Florida, and is also found through Central America to South America. This species grows naturally in open fields or on rocky slopes, and flowers mainly in early spring but has been known to flower at other times of the year.

Bletilla

(Abbreviation – Ble.)

There are nine or 10 species of *Bletilla*. The genus is related to *Cymbidium*, and some species have at times been classified as a *Cymbidium*.

These terrestrial plants and rhizomes occur naturally in temperate eastern Asia. They are widely distributed in China and into South East Asia and Japan. In fact, the rhizomes of some species are often used in Chinese herbal medicine.

They are normally found growing on sloping dry well-drained ground, among grasses, at altitudes of 100 to 3300 metres.

Bletilla produces corm-like pseudobulbs and upright stems growing laterally from the base of back bulbs.

The leaves are plicate (i.e. folded into plaits) and thin; flower racemes emerge from the tips of foliage. Petals and sepals are similar in appearance, and the 3-lobed lip is separate. This genus is very similar to the North American genus *Bletia* (see above) and is related to *Calanthe*.

Culture

This deciduous plant is adaptable to most soils, but likes a light, fertile loam. It will tolerate full sun, but needs protection from the heat of the day. It can be grown easily outside or as a pot plant. Propagate this orchid by division.

Cultivars

B. sinensis is similar to the more commonly grown *B. striata*, but has smaller dark red to rose flowers with darker makings on the sepals, petals and lip. It usually flowers in early summer.

B. striata (syn *B. hyacintha*) is capable of growing to 30 cm tall. The flowers are often pale purple – although the tone may vary – and may reach 3-5 cm across. Although *B. striata* are relatively cold-hardy, they need to be sheltered from extreme cold when grown in temperate regions. A white flowering variety is also grown in some countries. Most cultivars are bred from this species.

Brassavola

(Abbreviation – B.)

Consisting of 15-20 species, *Brassavola* are mainly epiphytes, with some lithophytes, and are related to *Cattleya*.

These orchids are native to the tropical Americas, and the stem-like pseudobulbs produce a solitary fleshy terminal leaf. The pseudobulbs can vary in shape.

Most *Brassavola* have narrow fleshy cylindrical or linear leaves which can sometimes be flattened and leathery.

Flower stems on short terminal racemes carry 1-3 blooms. Some species have fragrant flowers.

Culture

Brassavola prefer lots of water during their growth phase, but like dry conditions once they are established. Some species grow naturally in relatively dry, almost desert, conditions. Most differ from the majority of other orchid genera in that they do not like high humidity. They need a rest from watering in winter.

Grow in very well-drained baskets or pots in a chunky, open and dryish medium (a *Cattleya* medium is appropriate), or on cork bark. Roots rarely go deep and are normally sparse over the surface of the pot. Avoid heavy shade. The minimum night temperature in winter should be 13°C, and maximum day temperatures in summer around 24°C.

Propagate by division from large plants only.

The most common species of *Brassavola* is *B. nodosa*, which was originally identified as an *Epidendrum*.

Cultivars

B. acaulis develops leaves to 70 cm long, and has large fragrant greenish-white flowers.

B. cordata has leaves to around 25 cm with white to greenish-white fragrant flowers.

B. cucullata produces solitary white flowers to approximately 10 cm across, and cylindrical fleshy leaves to 30 cm long.

B. fragrans produces white to yellowish flowers with purple spots in early autumn.

B. glauca (syn. *Laelia glauca*) has bluish-grey leaves to around 12 cm long, and single fragrant pale green to white or purplish flowers.

B. nodosa has stem-like pseudobulbs which bear bluish-green leaves to around 20-40 cm long; the deliciously night-fragrant white to greenish flowers are up to 8 cm across.

B. Perrinii is a tuft-forming orchid with white to greenish flowers with green veins, yellow-green throat and a heart-shaped lip.

Brassia

(Abbreviation – Brs.)

This genus of epiphytes consists of 30-50 species from tropical America.

The pseudobulbs arise from thick creeping rhizomes and each has 1-3 leathery leaves.

The leaf shape varies and the flowers are on lateral racemes, growing from the base of pseudobulbs. Plant size can vary greatly according to the species. Most flower in summer, although some do in autumn. Petals and sepals of *Brassia* are narrow, long and pointed, sometimes appearing as spider-like flowers. The lip is entire (without lobes) and shorter than the sepals.

Culture

In cultivation, *Brassia* need a very open-rooted situation. They are best grown either in a very coarse chunky potting medium or attached to pieces of wood or tree fern, or in an open basket rather than in a pot. Aerial roots will grow over the surface and the outside of the container or attachment. Divide and repot only when necessary. *Brassia* are best grown in a greenhouse with high humidity and partial light exposure. *B. verrucosa* has succeeded in cooler condititions, but all *Brassia* prefer a minimum temperature of 15°C. They need a consistent source of water.

Cultivars

There are many species in cultivation.

B. arcuigera produces flowers with elongated green-brown petals and sepals with distinctive deep tan markings. The lip is cream with tan spots.

B. caudata has leaves to 15 cm long and greenish-yellow flowers with dark brown spots.

B. Gireoudiana is a large plant with leaves to 40 cm in length, and pseudobulbs to 12 cm long. Flower colours are variable, but tend to be brown, red-brown and yellow.

B. lanceana produces leaves to 30 cm long; flowers are variable, but are usually yellow with brown spots and a cream to white lip.

B. Lawrenciana has leaves to 20 cm long and fragrant yellow or greenish flowers with dark spots.

B. maculata (syn. *B. guttata*) produces yellow-green flowers with brown spots and leaves are typically up to 30 cm long.

B. verrucosa (syn. *B. brachiata*) is probably the most commonly cultivated species and is sometimes crossed with the genus.

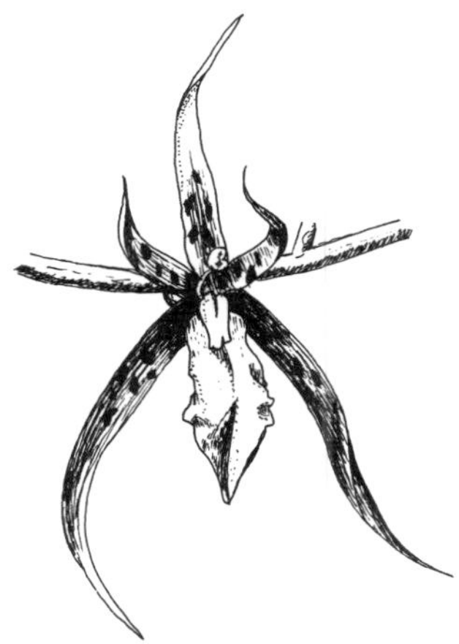

Brassia Lanceana

BULBOPHYLLUM

(Abbreviation – Bulb.)

Bulbophyllum is generally considered to be the biggest orchid genus, with approximately 1200 species (some say many more!). It consists of both large and tiny plants, deciduous as well as evergreen.

There are both tropical and temperate species, with around 40% coming from New Guinea and Irian Jaya. These tropical epiphytes or lithophytes grow as creeping rhizomes, developing pseudobulbs periodically.

The flowers vary, but all have a lip delicately jointed at the base. Occurring on one or more racemes or a leafless stem growing from the rhizome, the flowers have petals that are smaller than the sepals and host a thick fleshy lip, not obviously lobed and sometimes fringed. *Bulbophyllum* form a clump of stem-like pseudobulbs, usually with one broad fleshy leaf (occasionally two) at the top of each pseudobulb.

Culture

Most *Bulbophyllum* prefer minimum temperatures of 12°C or higher. A few will tolerate colder situations. The fleshy leaves can burn if they are not shaded from the sun.

Many grow well in shallow containers in a chunky coarse well-drained epiphytic potting medium (i.e. containing plenty of organic material). Water and feed during growth periods, usually late spring and summer, but do so conservatively as the plants react badly to overwatering or overfeeding.

Deciduous species have hard pseudobulbs, are mainly native to temperate areas, and need a period of dryness to rest each year. Tropical species need less of a rest period and should never dry out completely. Sub-tropical Asian species need a 2-week drying-out period after growth matures.

Propagate this orchid by division.

Cultivars

B. ambrosia (the Ambrosia Orchid) is a small plant with variable flower features, commonly white with red candy-stripe markings and a sweet scent. It is an epiphyte with a creeping rhizome.

B. basicetum produces deep blood-red flowers on a small plant.

B. Careyanum produces leaves to 20 cm long and large pseudobulbs on a thick rhizome. The flower stem develops a thick cluster of small yellow flowers with dark reddish markings and a purplish lip. The flowers have an unattractive smell, likened to rotting meat.

B. caudatum has long fine yellow to cream sepals, tiny petals and a 3-lobed cream to white lip which gives the flower a spider-like appearance. The pseudobulbs are a little over 1 cm long, topped with leaves to around 2.5 cm long.

B. graveolens (syn. *Cirrhopetalum graveolens*) produces a horizontal semicircle of off-white, or cream, and red flowers. The plant and flower are larger (and with different floral structural features) than a similar species called *B. longiforum*.

B. kwangtungensis is a small plant called the Antennae Orchid because of its relatively long, thin, spider-like sepals (up to 1.2 cm), making the flower 2.5 cm from top to bottom. Flowers are white and have a sweet fragrance. Leaves are flattened and up to 5 cm long and 1.4 cm wide.

B. leopardinum (the Leopard Orchid) produces a crowded cluster of tiny pseudobulbs carrying leaves to 12 cm long. Up to three drooping flowers arise from each pseudobulb on a short flower stem. The flowers can be 3 cm or more across, with broad (not spidery) petals and sepals, and are ochre-coloured and heavily spotted with red-purple. They look attractive but smell like rotten fruit, and attract flies.

B. lobbii produces a single attractive cream to brownish-yellow flower, with red or brown markings, on a stem to 10 cm long. The leaves are roughly elliptical and up to 35 cm long. Flowering can be intermittent at any time.

CALADENIA (SPIDER ORCHIDS)

(Abbreviation – Calda.)

The orchid genera *Caladenia* covers approximately 120 species, mainly from Australia, with a few species found in New Zealand and Asia. *Caladenia* are terrestrial and deciduous. The plant has a single basal leaf, normally hairy, that emerges from a pea-size tuberoid structure. Predominantly a spring flowering plant, the flower characteristics are variable, but all have a lip joined by a small claw to the base of the column. The lip is frequently 3-lobed, in which case the margins of the lateral lobes are often fringed. The size of the flowers can vary, but they are frequently conspicuous.

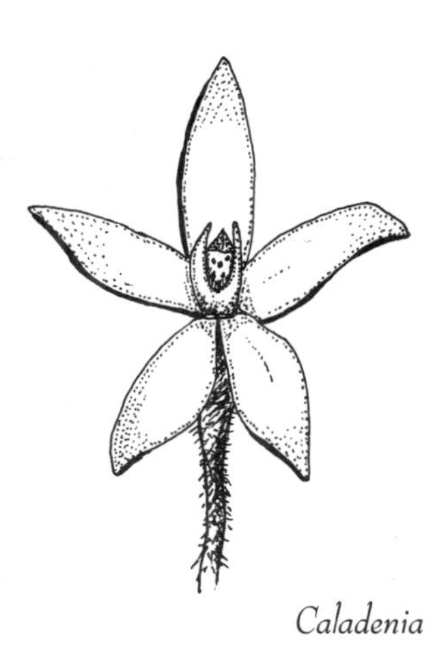

Caladenia

Culture

The natural habitat of the *Caladenia* species varies, but most thrive in well-drained soils and light shade in temperate regions. They are often found in open woodland. Generally speaking, they are difficult to cultivate and tend to deteriorate over two or more seasons to the point where flowering ceases.

Some species are virtually impossible to grow, with high humidity appearing to be the main problem in cultivation. Specialist growers in drier inland areas have had better results. Most species also have a delicate mycorrhizal relationship and need a potting mix containing eucalypt shavings or leaf mould to maintain mycorrhiza. Keep the soil moist, but never wet, while these plants are in growth and keep it dry when they are dormant.

Knowledge of the orchid's natural habitat will ensure that you can help the plant to survive in cultivation.

Cultivars

Caledanias are divided into two main groups: small-flowering forms and large-flowering.

SMALL FLOWERING FORMS

C. alata has a 6 cm leaf, and develops a white flower with some yellow on the lip.

C. aphylla produces cream-yellow flowers borne without a leaf present.

C. atroclavia has a hairy leaf and a pink flower with rose tones.

C. carnea typically develops a 15 cm leaf with pink flowers. Many variations occur including *C. carnea* var. *fuscata* – single white or pink flower 1.5 cm across; *C. carnea* var. *attenuata* – single white flower borne on stalks up to 24 cm tall; *C. carnea* var. *gigantea* – bright pink flowers up to 4.5 cm across borne on stalks up to 60 cm tall.

C. catenata carries white flowers above the 1.2 cm leaf.

C. latifolia produces 20 cm hairy leaves, and 1-4 bright pink flowers on stalks 40 cm tall.

C. menziesii develops a 9 cm ovate leaf. The white flowers are normally produced singly on 25 cm stalks, and display distinctive red glandular petals.

C. reptans has small pink flowers borne above the 5 cm leaf with a red underside.

LARGE FLOWERING FORMS

C. cairnsiana has a 12 cm leaf, and flowers yellowish-green or pinkish with red stripes, to 20 mm across.

C. caudata has 10 cm leaves with red spots at the base. The flowers are yellowish-green to 4 cm across and are suffused with red stripes.

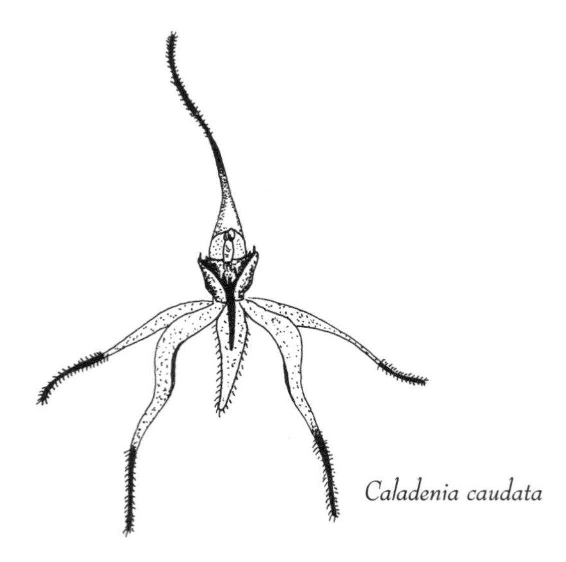

Caladenia caudata

C. denticulata produces a hairy 15 cm leaf, and 10 cm wide flowers with pale yellow petals with a red tinge.

C. ferruginea grows hairy 16 cm leaves, and flowers 6 cm across which are rusty red to red-brown.

C. lobata develops a hairy 15 cm leaf. The flowers attain 7 cm in diameter on stems 50 cm tall. They are yellow-cream with maroon markings.

C. pallida has 18 cm long hairy leaves. The flowers are pale greenish-yellow up to 7 cm across.

C. patersonii produces a 15 cm long leaf, and the cream-yellow flowers with red stripes are up to 8 cm across.

C. reticulata carries 12 cm hairy leaves beneath greenish-cream flowers suffused with crimson, and 6 cm across.

CALANTHE

(Abbreviation – Cal.)

Calanthe is another large genus, with approximately 150 species. They occur in a widespread area, from Central America to the Carribean, Pacific, Australasia and Asia. The plants are typically terrestrial; a few are epiphytic, with pseudobulbs. The pseudobulbs are normally inconspicuous, but can occasionally be large. The leaves are broad and sometimes deciduous, and some species shed foliage before flowering or during dry or very cold periods. Flowers occur on racemes or upright leafless stems, and the lip is a claw united to the column and usually 3-lobed.

Culture

Calanthe need a warm greenhouse with minimum temperatures of 12-15°C.

High humidity can lead to fungal problems and general deterioration resulting in a shortened life. Deciduous species should be given shade and lots of moisture when growing, but after the foliage goes, they need to be kept cool and dry. Evergreen species require more cool shade and should not be allowed to dry out. Watering is best done on the morning of a warm day. Do not water prior to colder weather.

Calanthe love shade; they are more prone to insect and mite attack than many other orchids. They respond well to frequent feeding, but avoid over-fertilising: use only slow-release fertiliser, otherwise there is a risk of burning the roots.

Evergreen species are propagated by division in spring. Deciduous species usually develop a new pseudobulb from each older bulb, which can be separated from the old plant in spring if the pseudobulbs are sound and vigorous.

Cultivars

C. *biloba* is an evergreen with foliage to 80 cm tall. Flowers are purplish with white markings.

C. *furcata* is an evergreen with foliage 70 cm tall. Flowers are on dense spikes to 1 m long, with each flower beginning cream or white and possibly turning blue.

C. *Masuca* is an evergreen with blue to yellow-green foliage. Flowers are violet to pale mauve, each to 2.5 cm long, borne with many on the one tall upright spike.

C. *rosea* is a deciduous orchid capable of growing to 45 cm tall. It has large pink to rose-coloured flowers.

C. *triplicata* is an evergreen plant with dark green pleated leaves and a tall flower spike up to 1.5 m with pure white flowers, each 3 cm across.

C. *vestita* is deciduous and up to 50 cm tall. The flowers are variable but are usually cream or white with a yellow to reddish centre. Several named cultivars are grown.

Hybrids

Many hybrids are cultivated.

CATTLEYA

(Abbreviation – C.)

There are approximately 60 species of *Cattleya*, mainly epiphytic, occurring naturally in a wide variety of habitats in tropical America. Some are lithophytic.

Cane-like pseudobulbs arise from creeping rhizomes, and each pseudobulb has 1-3 (rarely four) very stiff, thick leaves. The flowers are borne on racemes emerging from a terminal flower stem, which may carry several flowers or only one.

These variable and often very brightly coloured blooms are frequently large, with petals that are broader than the sepals, sepals that are similar to each other, and a 3-lobed lip.

Culture

One of the most popular orchids grown in warm climates or in greenhouses in cooler areas, *Cattleya* do best at temperatures from 13-30°C, in at least 50% humidity, and with indirect light and plenty of air movement.

Most *Cattleya* like as much indirect sunlight as possible in cool climates, but will require shading in warmer climates or over a hot summer. If the foliage is pale, increased shade may be needed. In too much shade, however, foliage can become lush and dark green. Such foliage is more susceptible to disease and the plant is less likely to flower. A medium, light green foliage is best on a *Cattleya*.

If you are impatient for flowers, buy plants with at least 5-8 pseudobulbs on them. Smaller plants can take years to flower.

When the plant is overgrown in its pot – potbound – you can partly cut the rhizome attached to the pseudobulb and leave it until new growth appears on it, or completely sever the pseudobulb and plant it separately from the rest of the plant immediately. Each new plant should have three or more pseudobulbs.

Unlike some orchids, *Cattleya* generally do not have that dormant period when the plants need to be drier. The roots need to be moist all year round, but never over-wet. On hot days they are best watered in the early morning, and allowed to dry out through the day. Large established plants often need watering only once each week. With high humidity, warm temperatures and good ventilation, disease problems are less likely. A small fan can be used 24 hours a day to keep air moving around the plants. Reduce watering in winter, but do not allow the stems to shrivel or shrink through dryness.

Thousands of hybrid *Cattleya* have been bred by crossing one species of *Cattleya* with another, or with other closely related groups of orchids. Resulting plants often have spectacular flowers 15cm across or more, in colours ranging from browns and reds to yellows, purples and whites.

Orchid growers commonly use abbreviations to designate *Cattleya* hybrids, as the names can become quite long and complicated. Most hybrids with *Cattleya* in the parentage have similar growing requirements to pure *Cattleya*.

Cultivars

Cattleya species fall into two groups. The following comments are generally true for each group.

- Single-leaved forms have only one leaf arising from the pseudobulb. Pseudobulbs are a medium size, swollen and well spaced. Flowers are particularly large, but rarely more than four in number, opening in succession over 2-3 weeks.
- Multiple-leaved forms normally have two leaves, or sometimes three (rarely four). These have thinner pseudobulbs which can be either very short or

very long, according to the species. There can be many flowers on a spike, up to 20 in some species.

C. Aclandiae is an epiphyte. It has 2-leaved pseudobulbs that vary from 1 cm to 1 m long. The petals and sepals are a greenish yellow with dark spots and the short lip is pale rose. *C. Aclandiae* Nigrescens is similar but with very dark brown petals and sepals.

C. aurantiaca (syn. *Epidendrum aurantiaca*) is naturally epiphytic. It produces the smallest *Cattleya* flowers, to only 4 cm across. The flower colour is variable, but commonly rich shades of orange to red. The pseudobulbs are 2-leaved and the plant can reach 30 cm in height.

C. Bowringiana is a 2-leaved type which is terrestrial in the wild, growing on rock or sand. Flowers are variable but are often in shades of rich pink with darker lip and throat markings. There are several named cultivars grown, each one different.

C. labiata (Autumn Cattleya) is an epiphyte from Brazil. It flowers in autumn to early spring, and has only one leaf to each pseudobulb. *C. labiata* has flowers to 15 cm across, which have variable characteristics. The petals and sepals are commonly pale rose to purplish, with colour variation in the lip. There are a number of well-known cultivars which are sometimes included within this species, and considered by other authorities as separate species (including *C. labiata* Mendelii , *C. labiata* Mossiae and *C. labiata* Percivaliana).

C. Leopoldii (syn. *C. guttata* var. *Leopoldii*) can have two or three leaves to a pseudobulb. Flowers are up to 10 cm across, brown to green with reddish purple dots and a predominantly white lip. In the past it was considered a variety of *C. guttata,* but is now recognised by many authorities as a separate species.

C. luteola has one leaf per pseudobulb, yellow flowers sometimes striped, and up to approximately 5 cm across. The lip is pale to white with a wavy margin. *C. luteola* is a relatively small *Cattleya*, rarely more than 15 cm tall, which is sometimes used to breed dwarf hybrids. It is best grown as an epiphyte, mounted on a slab.

C. maxima occurs naturally both as an epiphyte high in trees, and as a lithophyte on limestone outcrops. The pseudobulbs grow to 30 cm long, with one leaf. There are 3-15 flowers on a raceme; they can be up to 12 cm across, predominantly pale lilac to rose, with a light red to purplish lip marked with dark veins and an orange-yellow patch. Types originating from higher altitudes differ from those from lowland sites.

C. Mossiae is a large plant with pseudobulbs to 40 cm or longer and leaves to 20 cm long. There are usually three or four large flowers, up to 18 cm across, to a flower stem. There are many different varieties,with flowers varying from rich pink or lilac to white. The inside of the lip usually has darker markings.

C. warscewiczii has one leaf per pseudobulb. It produces some of the largest flowers of all *Cattleya*, up to 20 cm across. There are several varieties which were more commonly cultivated in the past than they are today. The blooms usually have a strong pleasant scent, pale purple petals and sepals, and a dark purplish lip bearing lighter markings.

Hybrids

Cattleya hybrids are divided mainly into the following groups.

- *Cattleya* hybrids are plants arising from only *Cattleya* parents, e.g. *C.* Earl × *C.* Princess Belle,which develops plump frilled white petals and a yellow centre, and *C.* Bahiana, which produces yellow sepals with red-brown spots, and suffused pink petals.
- *Laeliocattleya* are plants arising from *Laelia* and *Cattleya* hybrids. These are generally free flowering, with flowers not quite as large as *Cattleya*; colours are yellows, oranges and greenish to lavender.
- *Brassocattleya* are plants arising from *Cattleya* and *Rhyncholaelia* hybrids. (NB: *Rhyncholaelia* are species which were originally included under *Brassavola*, but which are a little more tolerant of heat and dryness than other *Brassavola*. Some still call them by this name.)
- *Brassolaeliocattleya* have parents which include *Laelia*, *Rynocholaelia* and *Cattleya*. This name is commonly abbreviated to *Blc*. Colours are rich and bright, similar to *Laelia* and the large ruffled lip is similar to *Rhyncholaelia*.
- *Sophralaeliocattleya* have parents which include *Sophronitis*, *Laelia* and *Cattleya*. This name is abbreviated to *Slc*. This is a relatively new group, generally suiting cooler conditions than some of the other *Cattleya* hybrids. Vibrant flower colours range from yellows through oranges to reds and purples.
- *Pontinaria* are produced with parents from four different genera: *Cattleya*, *Laelia*, *Rhyncholaelia* and *Sophronitis*.

There are dozens of other intergeneric *Cattleya* hybrids and each has approved and registered abbreviations such as those above. The five above, however, are the most widely cultivated.

COELOGYNE

(Abbreviation – Coel.)

Native to tropical Asia, South East Asia and the Pacific region, the *Coelogyne* genus consists of approximately 200 species of plants. They are epiphytes and have pseudobulbs that arise at intervals along rhizomes, each normally with two dark green spoon-shaped and very thick leaves. The leaves are linear to elliptical and are rolled when young. Showy long-lasting flowers in racemes are commonly 2-3 cm in diameter and usually appear in pale colours: shades of cream, brown, green or beige. The lip is usually 3-lobed, and concave at the base. *Coelogyne* flower stems are erect to pendant and in many cases the blooms are fragrant.

Culture

Coelogyne prefer a shady cool position. Ventilation, light and moisture need to be carefully managed to achieve best results, so the plants may have to be moved about to get conditions right throughout the year. Generally, most are better suited to mild temperate conditions than to sub-tropics. They need lots of water when actively growing, but water lying on buds or leaves will lead to fungal problems.

The potting mix needs to be modified to suit the plant's environmental conditions and the species being grown. Pot into chunky bark and charcoal with some finer organic material to feed roots and hold moisture.

Don't pot up too often, as most species need to be potbound to flower. Only repot in spring when roots are just beginning to grow.

There are two main groups of *Coelogyne*. The Himalayan *Coelogyne* do best in cool conditions and need a rest period over winter. They prefer temperatures at or below 25°C. The tropical *Coelogyne* grow well all year round, but are cold-sensitive. Minimum temperature should be 15°C. Good drainage is essential, and they really need to be either mounted on bark or planted in a hanging basket to do well.

Cultivars

C. barbarata is a Himalayan species with leaves to 50 cm long, and up to 10 mainly white flowers clustered densely on a stem to 60 cm tall.

C. dayana can grow to 75 cm tall, with up to 50 yellowish to brown to yellow, or white, flowers on a stem. One cultivated plant was recorded in 1893 with 24 flower spikes and over 800 flowers. Tropical species such as this grow well in an open slat basket.

C. cristata will develop pseudobulbs in a raised clump, one on top of another. The species needs to be overgrown (potbound) like this to flower. The flowers are scented and pure white with a yellow keel. Several named varieties exist, with generally minor variations in flower colour. Many experienced orchid growers produce healthy plants of this species, but flowers elude them. It is a Himalayan species.

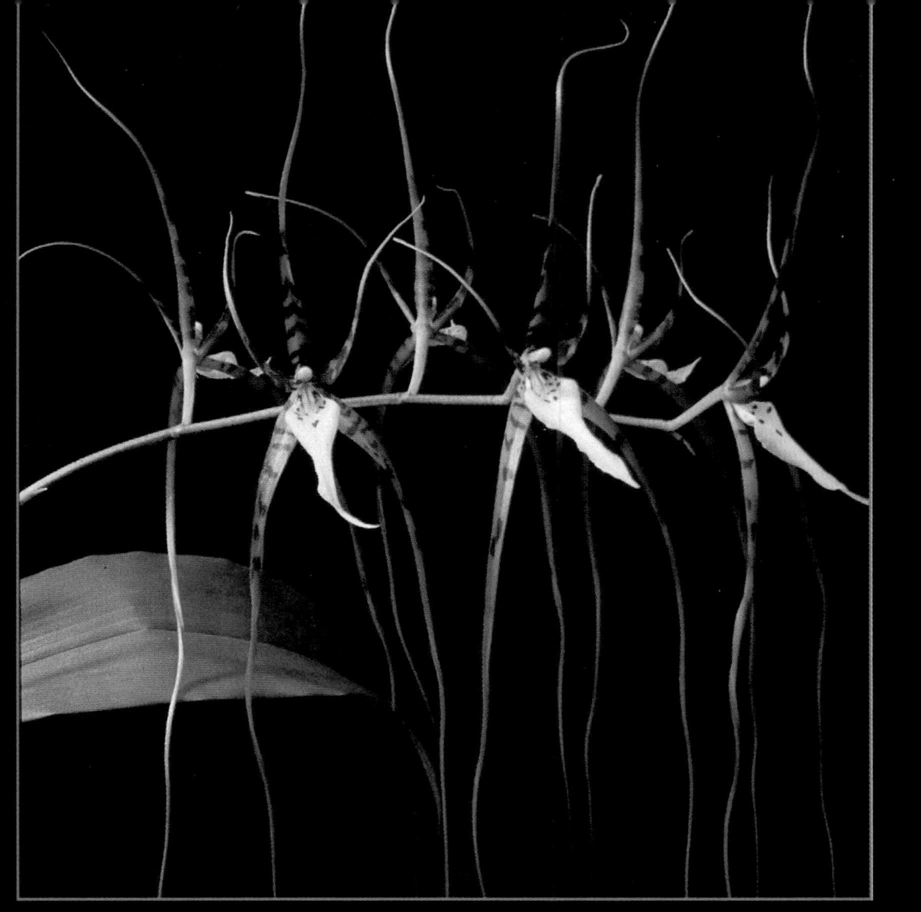

Brassia arcuigera PHOTO: GARY YONG GEE

Pleione cultivar

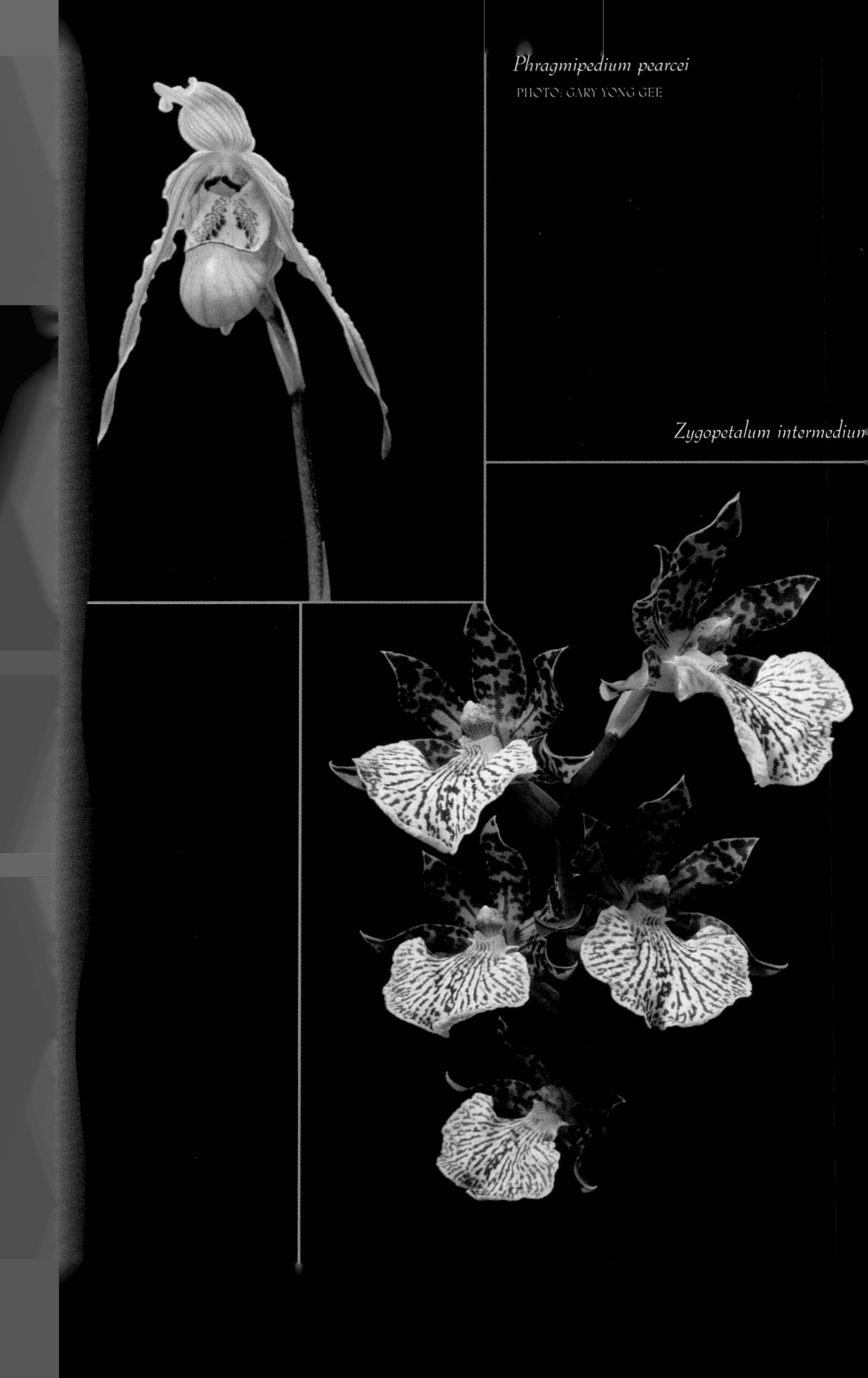

Phragmipedium pearcei
PHOTO: GARY YONG GEE

Zygopetalum intermedium

C. Massangeana is a tropical type, with leaves to 60 cm long. It normally produces pale yellow flowers with brown, yellow and white marking. This orchid grows best in an open slat basket.

C. pandurata (Black Orchid) produces very attractive black and green flowers, but it does tend to outgrow its container and then rapidly deteriorate. Leaves grow around 60 cm long. It is a tropical type.

C. speciosa is relatively easy to grow, with leaves to almost 40 cm tall. It produces flowers to 10 cm across, with yellow-green or brownish green petals, and a reddish-brown or pale yellowish lip. This is a tropical species.

CORYBAS (HELMET ORCHID)

The *Corybas* genus, commonly known as Helmet Orchids, include approximately 100 species. Their native habitat is found in Asia through to Australasia. Most are from temperate regions, but one is from Macquarie Island in the Arctic Ocean, and four others are native to the tropics. These very small terrestrial orchids, with one broad rounded leaf that sits on the soil surface, produce a single flower that grows on a thick short stem. The dorsal sepal is very large and dominates the flower. The lip can have hairs or teeth (fringed) or be smooth.

Helmet Orchid

Culture

In nature, *Corybas* grow mostly in colonies in sheltered positions protected by other plants, such as grasses or herbs, or in open woodland. Cultivation is relatively easy for the species, which form colonies in the wild. Dryness or low humidity can cause developing flower buds to abort. Covering individual plants with plastic can maintain humidity as flowers develop and overcome this problem. Species that do not occur in colonies tend to deteriorate in cultivation.

All are deciduous and become dormant in dry hot summers, dying down to the underground tuber. With autumn rain, the tuber sprouts a new leaf.

The flower is a dominant hooded dorsal sepal, and lip, with other floral parts almost reduced to minor appendages. The lamina (leaf blade) is usually adorned with small hairs or soft teeth, but can be smooth.

Cultivars

Easy to grow species include the following.

C. aconitiflorus has an erect purplish flower on a short stalk.

C. despectans produces reddish purple and green sessile flowers (no flower stalk).

C. diemenicus has veined dark reddish and white flowers, with a distinct toothed lip, on a short stalk.

C. fimbriatus flowers are sessile, dark reddish purple with a semi-translucent hood, and toothed lip.

C. hispidus has a dark reddish-purple dorsal petal with purple spots. The lip has a characteristic white centre and is coarsely toothed.

C. incurvis has a stalked flower with a greenish-grey hood and purple spots. The lip has purple margins, a white raised centre and a few short teeth.

C. macranthus produces a greenish dorsal sepal (hood), and a dark purple lip covered with small teeth.

C. neocaledonicus has a dark maroon flower on small slender stalk, and the dorsal sepal covers most of the rest of flower. The lip is minutely-toothed.

C. pruinosus has a flower that is short-stalked or sessile. The hood is greyish with purple streaks, the lip is mostly rounded and smooth with coarse teeth.

Cymbidium

(Abbreviation – Cym.)

There are approximately 50 species native to tropical Asia and Australia. Most are terrestrial, but some are epiphytes.

Cymbidium produce pseudobulbs, which can be large, or in some cases very small, even insignificant. Each pseudobulb of a healthy plant will have many leaves under good conditions. These leaves are normally long, narrow and thick, but can sometimes vary. The plants grow continuously, without the quiescent or resting period that is typical of other orchids. Appearing on lateral racemes, the flowers of this plant have petals and sepals that are similar and a lip that varies from entire to 3-lobed.

The *Cymbidium* genus is a very diverse group, with an immense number of hybrids and varieties. Some *Cymbidium* are more cold tolerant than *Cattleya*, withstanding temperatures of around 7°C. In the cooler southern regions of Australia, such as Melbourne and Adelaide, many people have outstanding success with *Cymbidium* grown in a shadehouse, on a verandah or under a protective large tree.

Some growers separate *Cymbidium* into two groups: those from warm zones and those from temperate-cold zones.

Culture

Cymbidium should not be watered over winter; in wet areas some people turn pots on the side for a while to stop the roots becoming too wet and rotting. Watering in the evening in summer drops the root temperature for the night, which in turn helps initiate flowering. In very hot late summer conditions, apply a weak epsom salts solution to *Cymbidium* once a week. Feed regularly over spring and autumn, but not through late summer: being short on nutrients in January/February helps promote flowering. Potting media needs to be well drained, preferably a mix made specifically for *Cymbidium*.

Flower spikes develop over winter and bloom throughout the spring. Frost during these times will bleach and distort flowers, and can even kill the plant. Plants prefer winter minimums to 10°C and summer maximums of 24-27°C, but will tolerate a much wider temperature range. Many of the modern hybrids prefer temperatures around 20-27°C over summer. *Cymbidium* will perform better if winter temperatures can be kept around 10°C and those growers in colder climates should consider bringing their plants indoors over winter. In hot summer districts, light shading (to 30%), or light watering or misting, may be required to cool the plants.

All *Cymbidium* prefer indirect sunlight, particularly once flowers open. However, some are more sun-tolerant than others. Of all orchids, *Cymbidium* tend to tolerate the most direct sunlight, especially in the growing phase before flowering begins. Pink or red flowering *Cymbidium* tolerate brighter light than green flowering types. Yellow and white flowering varieties vary in their light tolerance. Yellow or green varieties produce more vibrant flowers if greater shade is provided. Return to better light conditions after flowering.

Flowers are long lasting. A spike can easily last for six weeks. Flowering is thought to be initiated by long bright days combined with cool nights. Flower initiation occurs in mid to late summer in all *Cymbidium* species, but actual flowering time will depend on the cultivar. Maximum flowering is achieved when the summer day temperature is 21°C and night is 14°C.

Every variety of *Cymbidium* needs to reach a certain size before it will flower. This varies from one variety to the next. One may require three mature bulbs, another three times that number. Plants can be grown from back bulbs (pseudobulbs), similar to the way *Cattleya* are propagated. With *Cymbidium*, however, one pseudobulb is sufficient for a new plant. When dividing, dust any cuts with fungicide (e.g. sulphur) to minimise the chance of rotting.

Bulb rot is common if pots get over-wet in summer. Control with a Fongarid drench. Black leaf spot often occurs and can be controlled with a Mancozeb spray. If the summer is dry, bulb rot is unlikely, but mites could be a problem. Other pest and disease problems include:

- Mealy bugs: these cluster around the pseudobulbs; use a systemic insecticide (e.g. Omethoate or Confidor).
- Scale: you will find these at lower sections of the plant; use a systemic insecticide.
- Red spider mites: these cause silvering of leaves, delicate webbing and, a more minor symptom, misshapen leaves; use a miticide, discard infected plants or introduce biological control agents.
- Aphids: these insects suck the sap from healthy new shoots and flowers; control with pyrethrum or another appropriate insecticide.
- Leaf spots: these are commonly caused by fungal diseases; control by removing infected leaves or, in extreme cases, by spraying with a fungicide (e.g. Mancozeb). Some streaks and spots may be caused by viral infection. Virus-infected plants are best isolated, or even destroyed.
- Leaf tip browning: this is caused by water stress and high fertiliser content; improved cultural practices are probably the best solution.
- *Cymbidium* mosaic virus: mild infections may be similar to leaf spots; as it develops it causes distortion and discolouration; dispose of infected plants.

Cultivars

Some species *Cymbidium* are grown; however, most cultivated *Cymbidium* are either 'standard' hybrids or miniatures.

There are many regular hybrids that can reach a height of more than 1.5 m, with a single spike carrying as many as 30 flowers. Miniatures naturally are smaller plants with lower foliage and smaller flowers.

Miniatures generally like to be watered all year round, while the larger hybrids often like to have a period of dryness. Miniatures also tend to be more resilient in hotter temperatures.

There are more than 50 recorded *Cymbidium* species.

C. canaliculatum is a dense plant with 2-6 thick deeply channelled leaves per pseudostem. It has fragrant flowers that vary from pale green to reddish-black and appear in racemes of five or up to 60.

C. *eburneum* has diminished or insignificant pseudobulbs, leaves to 60 cm long and an upright flower stem carrying only 1-3 flowers. The flowers are fragrant and mainly ivory white. The lip is white with a yellow centre. There are named varieties in which the flowers vary both in colour and shape.

C. elegans produces thick pseudobulbs, narrow leaves to 70 cm long, and a dense spike of 4 cm-diameter flowers, commonly brownish-yellow with red dots on the lip.

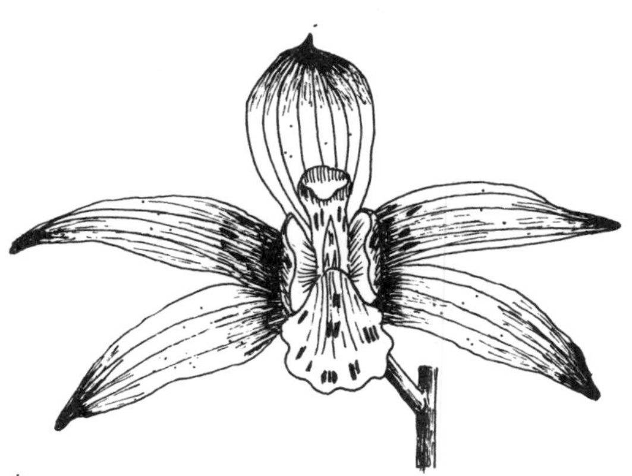

Cymbidium giganteum

C. giganteum has arching linear leaves to 70 cm long, and ovoid pseudobulbs. Flower spikes carry up to 15 flowers, each to 10 cm across, commonly green to brownish-yellow and fragrant.

C. grandiflorum has leaves to 70 cm long and flower stems to 1 m long. The flowers are fragrant, are up to 10 cm across and variable in colour, often greenish or yellowish with darker markings.

C. insigne has been grown extensively as a species, and as a parent for hybridisation with other species. It has spherical pseudobulbs, leaves 50 cm-1 m or longer. As many as 15 flowers, each to 10 cm across, can occur on each flowering spike. Flower colour is variable but often the blooms are pale rose to lilacwith a darker lip in the centre. *C. insigne* Album has a white lip with green markings.

C. Lowianum grows 60-90 cm tall. Each flower spike can carry up to 25 flowers, 10 cm in diameter. A number of cultivars exist, and flower colour can be variable; however, flowers are commonly fragrant, greenish with brown veins, and a yellow and red marked central lip.

C. madidum is a large clumped plant with thin dark green leaves. Racemes (flower stems) can reach 60 cm long and carry 70 fragrant flowers. Flower colour varies from pale- to brown-green.

C. pumilum is a dwarf species which has been used to produce some miniature *Cymbidium*. Its leaves reach 30 cm, and flowers of up to 3 cm across occur on a dense spike. Flowers are commonly white to pinkish with reddish markings, but there are variations, including *C. pumilum* 'Shuo-Lan', which has green to brown sepals and a yellow lip with red markings.

C. sauva produces long grass-like leaves with fragrant brownish-green flowers borne on 30 cm long racemes.

C. zygopetalum produces vibrant pink-purple and brown flower parts.

Hybrids

There are countless hybrids of *Cymbidium* grown throughout the world, and new ones are being released constantly. It is largely pointless to refer in any detail to specific hybrids, given that the choice is so diverse. The following are, however, just some of the older hybrids that are often referred to in literature.

C. × *Alexanderi* is a hybrid of *C. Veitchii* and *C. insigne*. Flowers reach 10 cm across and may be white, cream or bluish pink. This hybrid has been used extensively for breeding other cultivars.

C. × *Veitchii* is a hybrid of *C. eburneum* and *C. Lowianum*, and it has large fragrant flowers to 12 cm across.

Cypripedium

(Abbreviation – Cyp.)

There are 30-50 species in this genus, which is related closely to *Paphiodedilum* and *Phragmipedium*. Classification has often been confused between this and other genera (e.g. *Selenipedium* has often been included in this genus).

Cypripediums are known to occur from sub-arctic to sub-tropical areas in the northern hemisphere. Most are north of latitude 35° north.

These terrestrial plants are deciduous, with the foliage dying back to the rhizome in winter. They commonly grow in woodland or meadows and typically have a long leafy stem rather than a fan of basal leaves growing from a rhizome. The lower stem is hairless. Height can vary a great deal, from 10 cm (in full flower) to 1.5 m tall. Cypripedium flower in spring or summer. The flowers are white with pinkish to purplish mottled colourings on the pouch (the lip of the flower extends to form a sac or pouch).

Cypripedium macranthum

Culture

Many *Cypripedium* grow well in the open ground in temperate climates. Most prefer well-drained, high organic soil, and must be protected from severe frost or snow. Species which occur naturally in snow-prone areas become dormant over winter, and the roots are covered with snow. In such situations, growth should not begin until all snow has gone. A flush of growth followed by a late fall of snow can be fatal. Otherwise most *Cypripedium* are hardy.

Rhizomes often branch, which allows propagation by division.

Cultivars

C. acaule (Pink Lady's Slipper) has solitary flowers, reddish purple with a pinkish lip. It is extremely hardy in cooler climates (growing well in Britain), and needs acidic soil.

C. Calceolus has foliage up to 70 cm tall. The shape and colour of flowers can be variable (yellow-green to purplish or brownish is common). It is perhaps the most commonly grown species with many different named cultivars. Varieties occur naturally from Texas to the Yukon in the north of Canada.

C. Calceolus pubescens (Yellow Lady's Slipper) produces solitary green yellow flowers, with yellow lip/pouch.

C. candidum grows to 30 cm tall, and produces solitary flowers on a stem. Sepals and petals are greenish with dark markings and the lip is white with purple spots.

C. macranthum produces solitary blooms; dorsal sepal, petals and lip are pink to purple, lateral sepals greenish-brown.

C. reginae is particularly hardy, but is covered with hairs which can irritate the skin. It used in hybridisation with *Phragmipedium*. It grows to around 80 cm tall; the petals and sepals are white, and the lip is white with purplish or reddish markings.

Hybrids

Some hybrids are grown, including *C* × *Andrewsii* which is produced from *C. candidum*x × *C. Calceolus parvifolium*.

DENDROBIUM

(Abbreviation – Den.)

Mainly from tropical and sub-tropical Asia, the Pacific and Australia, *Dendrobium* is another very large genus of orchids, with approximately 900 or more species included. The foliage is very variable; it can be very leafy and may have either few stems, or a lot; the flowers are also variable: there may be only one or many on a raceme. Almost all of the species in this genus are epiphytic.

Some moves has been made to reclassify some of the species. For example, *D. linguiforme*, *D. mortii* and *D. teretifolium* are sometimes reclassified under the new genera *Dockrillia*.

Culture

As a group, *Dendrobium* are diverse, both in how they look and how they need to be treated. Though most *Dendrobium* are epiphytes and many need to be grown on a slab of fern or timber, some will grow quite well in a pot.

There are *Dendrobium* which can be grown in all types of climates, from the tropics to cool temperate areas, though most come from mild or warm climates. If we were to generalise, the most important requirement is fresh air or good ventilation, followed by appropriate shade. Overwatering is always a danger with *Dendrobium* grown in pots.

Many can be grown by division of offsets or separation. The pseudobulbs are commonly elongated and look like a piece of cane, hence are commonly called canes.

Cultivars

There are several different ways of classifying *Dendrobium*; this is one way.

Soft cane – the cane is generally swollen or thick and soft inside.
Black hair (Nigro-hirsute) - canes are covered by short black hairs.
Hard cane – canes are thin and long.

Species	*Type*	*Requirements*	*Growing method*
D. adae	Hard cane	Shady site	Epiphyte
D. aemulum	hard cane	Shade to bright light	Epiphyte
D. aggregatum	Hard cane	Need long dry period	Very open mix
D. bellatulum	Black hair	Dry out over winter	Epiphyte-fern slab is ideal
D. bigibbum (Cooktown Orchid) (syn. *D. phalaenopsis*)	Hard cane	Prefers bright light grows all year round in warm climates	Pot or Epiphyte or lithophyte
D. bracteosum	Soft cane	Semi-shade	Pot or Epiphyte
D. canaliculatum	Hard cane	Bright light	Epiphyte
D. discolor	Hard cane	Bright light	Pot or epiphyte or lithophyte

Species	*Type*	*Requirements*	*Growing method*
D. falcorostrum	Hard cane	Shade to bright light	Epiphyte or in pots
D. formosum	Black hair	Very warm climates	Epiphyte
D. × gracillum	Hard cane	Bright light, cool humid conditions	Epiphyte or lithophyte
D. gracilicaule	Hard cane	Bright light	Epiphyte or lithophyte
D. johannis	Hard cane	Bright light, warm humid conditions	Epiphyte or in a pot
D. kingianum	Hard cane	Semi-shaded position	Pot or lithophyte
D. linguiforme	Hard cane	Very adaptable	Epiphyte
D. moorei	Hard cane	Semi-protected site Cool humid conditions	Epiphyte or lithophyte
D. mortii	Hard cane	Sub-tropic humid conditions	Epiphyte
D. nobile	Soft cane	At least 50% shade Needs a cool dry dormancy period of 1-2 months over winter	Epiphytic
D. smilliae	Hard cane	Tropics: hot, humid and bright light Allowed complete dry in winter	Epiphyte or lithophyte
D. speciosum (Sydney Rock Orchid)	Hard cane	Prefers bright light	Epiphyte or lithophyte
D. teretifolium	Hard cane	Good light, humidity and air movement	Epiphyte or lithophyte
D. tetragonum	Hard cane	Moist shady conditions	Epiphyte or lithophyte

Hybrids of the various species, and hybrids of these, have resulted in hundreds of cultivars.

Each exhibits unique features in flower form and colour, and growth hardiness.

Diuris

There are 40 species of *Diuris*, all of which come from Australia with one exception, and this is native to Timor. The plants are terrestrial and deciduous, and their foliage will die down over the dry part of summer to leave tuberoid roots which grow new foliage after the rain in autumn. Commonly, many plants grow together in a group or colony, often amongst grasses, and usually in soils that are wet or moist over winter.

Most species have 1-3 long thin grass-like leaves. A few reproduce vegetatively to grow a dense grass-like clump of leaves. The flowers occur on an erect raceme and have a distinctive and characteristic shape, the two sepals arranged to look like donkeys' ears.

Most species have yellow flowers, but some are in shades of pink to purple, and are considered to be relatively large for a small orchid, often 2 cm across. Some species are fragrant.

Culture

Diuris are relatively easy to grow and will flower readily in cultivation. Potting media should contain one third leaf mould or eucalypt shavings. When foliage begins to die down over summer, allow soil to dry out; start watering in winter, only when active growth begins. Repot every 2-3 years.

Most *Diuris* propagate relatively easily by seed or division of tubers. Hybridisation is not uncommon in the wild, sometimes making identification difficult.

Cultivars

D. abbreviata develops 3-9 pale yellow flowers with brown markings on a stalk up to 45 cm tall.

D. alba has 2-6 fragrant flowers on 35 cm stems. Flowers are white with lilac markings.

D. aurea has a 60 cm stem, with 3-7 flowers, clear yellow with darker markings.

D. chrysantha has a 30 cm stem bearing 2-7 golden-coloured flowers with brown markings.

D. corymbosa has 1-8 flowers on a 45 cm stem. They vary in size and colour but are usually yellow with darker markings. Growth needs to be confined (i.e. potbound) to encourage flowers.

D. lanceolata bears 1-4 lemon yellow flowers, with outer darker markings. The flower stem is 40 cm tall.

D. longifolia produces 1-6 purplish flowers with yellow markings on a 30 cm stem.

D. maculata has 2-8 yellow flowers heavily spotted with dark brown on a 30 cm stem.

D. punctata produces a 60 cm flower stem with up to 10 predominantly purple flowers. Flower features can vary, but normally include dark markings.

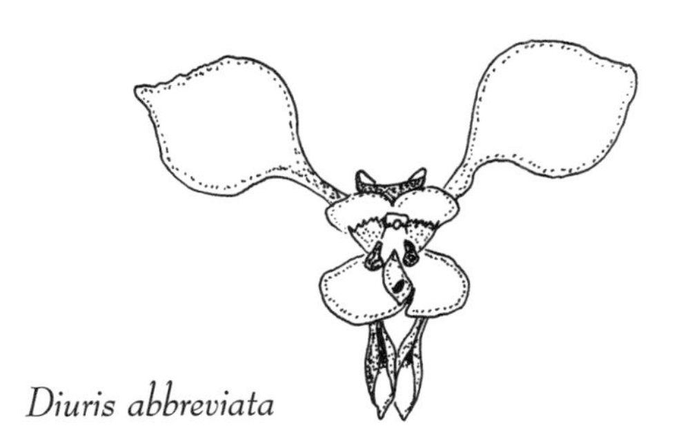

Diuris abbreviata

The flowers may or may not be fragrant depending on the form.

D. semilunulata has 3-5 orange-yellow flowers, heavily blotched with purple, on a 35 cm flower stem.

D. sulphurea produces up to seven yellow flowers with dark markings on a 60 cm stem. Tubers need restriction to encourage flower growth.

Doritis

(Abbreviation – Dor.)

Related to *Vanda* and *Phalaenopsis*, *Doritis* was originally known as *Phalaenopsis*. One reason for this is that the plant naturally occurs in similar conditions to Phalaenopsis. The flower colour can be quite variable and each flower spike can hold up to 20 or more flowers. Stems on a mature plant are generally taller than *Phalaenopsis*.

There are only two species, both epiphytes, from Asia and South East Asia.

Culture

In general, *Doritis* are slightly hardier than *Phalaenopsis*. They need to be provided with moderate shade, but will not tolerate heavy shade.

Fertilise with only weak liquid fertiliser and use a chunky open potting medium for best results. They can be grown in the same potting medium as *Phalaenopsis*. Unlike many orchids, the *Doritis* genus prefers to be grown in a pot.

Propagation is difficult as side shoots are rare to develop, providing scarce opportunity for division.

Cultivars

D. pulcherrima is a particularly robust species, normally flowering in autumn. It will survive periods of a month or more of hot dry conditions, discarding foliage which then regrows once conditions improve. Flower characteristics are quite variable: they are normally 2-3 cm across, commonly lilac or amethyst, with flower spikes to around 70 cm tall. The leaves are up to 20 cm long.

ENCYCLIA

Encyclia are native to Central and South America and the Carribean. The genus is often noted as synonymous with *Epidendrum*. Some botanists consider *Encyclia* to be *Epidendrum*. While the two are closely related, they do differ. *Encyclia* have distinct pseudobulbs topped by leaves, with flowering stems emerging from the centre of these, while *Epidendrum* do not have such definite pseudobulbs. The *Epidendrum* flower column is completely united with the labellum, while in the *Encyclia* the two are separate.

These orchids consist of pseudobulbs that form on extensions of the rhizomes. The flowers are often showy and very long lasting, and the flowering season ranges from summer to autumn.

Culture

Some plants will grow in containers, but most prefer to be grown on slabs. *Encyclia* do better if water is applied only to the back of the slab to keep the foliage and roots from being moistened.

Avoid potting up into too large a container or on to too big a slab. Instead, increase the size by one small step each time you repot.

A good potting medium is a predominantly chunky open mix of bark and charcoal, possibly with some stones and organic material (e.g. sphagnum).

The ideal temperature range should be a minimum of 13°C (winter night) to a maximum of 22°C (summer day). For most of this genus, it is best to provide a position similar to that for *Cattleya*, in terms of shade, light, temperature and ventilation (see *Cattleya*). Some species (e.g. *E. vitellina* and *E. citrina*) can be given cooler conditions.

Cultivars

E. cochleata produces flowers with a striped yellowish lip featuring green and dark purple markings. The ribbon-like petals and sepals are generally pale green, long, narrow and dangling. Plants can vary in size, with leaves normally 20-30 cm long. They need water all year.

E. cordigera (syn. *E. osmantha* or *Epidendrum atropurpureum*) is sometimes called the 'Spice Orchid'. It has greenish-brown flowers to 7.5 cm across, often tinged with purple, and a white lip with a reddish centre.

E. mariae has fragrant flowers which have a large white lip with green veins inside the centre. The lip dominates the light green petals and sepals. This species needs reduced watering over autumn and a dry period in winter.

E. oncidioides (syn. *Epidendrum odoratissimum*) has fragrant greenish flowers with yellow and red markings.

E. virens (syn. *Epidendrum diurnum*) has leaves to 45 cm and flower spikes to 80 cm. Flowers are greenish to yellow with purplish markings.

E*ncyclia radiata* has fragrant flowers.

EPIDENDRUM (CRUCIFIX ORCHIDS)

(Abbreviation – Epi.)

Over 1000 species make up the genus *Epidendrum*. They are most commonly epiphytes or lithophytes, and are native to the tropical and sub-tropical American continents. The stems are either elongated and leafy, or are pseudobulbs. The flowers are terminal and can occur singly in some species, but are more commonly in a cluster. Some species need warm humid conditions, while others will tolerate temperate climates quite well.

Culture

Crucifix orchids have masses of small flowers (normally shades of yellow, orange or red) with a cross-like section as part of the flower. Many are particularly easy to grow, adapting to climates as diverse as Singapore (tropical) to Melbourne (temperate). Growth and flowering, however, is less vigorous in cooler climates. In Australia, the commonly cultivated red flowering crucifix orchid (believed to be a variety of *E. ibaguense*), performs best in cooler areas. It also performs better than those varieties of a colour other than red

Epidendrum can be grown in well-drained garden beds or pots. They need plenty of organic matter to grow well, and are heavier feeders than many other orchids, responding to almost any quantity of well-rotted manure.

Many propagate easily from stem cuttings and cuttings of side shoots, while some produce pseudobulbs and can be propagated by division.

Cultivars

There are many species and hybrids in culture. The exact parentage of some cultivars is confused. Species are sometimes divided into reed-stemmed types and soft-stemmed species. There are a greater number of soft-stemmed species, but the reed-stemmed are hardier plants, easier to propagate, and much more commonly cultivated.

E. aromaticum has yellowish flowers, with a whitish lip and red markings. Flowers occur in spring to summer, and are strongly scented.

E. atropurpureum (Spice Orchid) has fragrant brownish flowers, with a white and purplish lip, in winter or early spring. This is an extremely variable species.

E. cinnabarinum needs minimum temperatures of 15°C or higher if it is to flower. Flowers occur from spring to summer and are bright scarlet, with an orange-yellow lip spotted with red.

E. fragrans is a small plant with scented flowers in winter or spring. Flowers are white with a purplish-streaked lip.

E. ibaguense (syn. *E. radicans*) is a typical reed-stemmed type, and perhaps the most commonly grown species of *Epidendrum*. It grows easily in cool, warm or hot climates, provided it has protection from frost. It will grow in the lowlands of Malaysia, and also outside in Melbourne. To flower well, it needs plenty of sun, and in temperate areas needs a warm open position that collects optimum sunlight. In such a situation it is unlikely to suffer sunburn. Climbing species have many aerial roots; the flowers are not scented, and may occur at any time.

E. medusae is a typical soft-stemmed type with fleshy blue-green leaves. Flowers are yellowish-green with brown, and have a large purplish lip. It needs both shade and warmth to do well.

E. Parkinsonianum (syn. *E. falcatum*) produces fragrant long-lasting flowers; their colour varies greatly. Keep fairly moist and allow only slight drying between waterings. Ideal conditions are temperatures of 10-27°C, with 55-75% humidity; feed weekly at 25-50% recommended rates. Mount plants on cork, bark or tree fern slabs or in a hanging pot in a chunky fast-draining medium.

E. radicans – see *E. ibaguense.*

E. Stamfordianum has yellow and red spotted fragrant flowers with a fringed lip, occurring in early summer or late autumn. This species can be temperamental in cultivation.

E. stenopetalum is another soft-stemmed species, producing a clump of cylindrical stems to 70 cm tall, bearing 10 cm leathery leaves. With appropriate conditions (e.g. shade and constant warmth) this species can produce predominantly rose to purplish flowers all year round.

Hybrids

Many interspecies and intergeneric hybrids have been developed. Hybrids between *Cattleya* and *Epidendrum* are grown in many places including tropical South East Asia.

Epiphronitis are developed from *Epidendrum* and *Sophronitis*. *Epicattleya* are hybrids of *Epidendrum* with *Cattleya*. Some authorities have abbreviated this as *Epc*. as opposed to *Epct*.

Auliza is synonymous with *Epidendrum*. Although many botanists would consider *Aulzia* to be the same genus as *Epidendrum*, in common usage *Auliza* is still applied.

GLOSSODIA (WAX LIP ORCHID)

Glossodia is one of the smaller types of orchids. There are only two species, both from eastern Australia: *G. major* is found from south-east Queensland to South Australia, and *G. minor* is found in Victoria, New South Wales and Queensland.

Glossodia are terrestrial and are indigenous to open forests and heathlands. The deciduous foliage dies down to the small tuberoids in the hot dry summer. Occurring as scattered single plants or in small groups, *Glossodia* have one dark green leaf per plant, arising from the base. The leaf is hairy.

Flowers occur mainly in spring and are brightly coloured and open very widely. The flower colour is commonly purple to mauve, but they are occasionally white.

Culture

Generally, this genus is not too difficult to cultivate, and can be long-lived. Always keep the soil moist, but never wet, while the plant is in growth. When the plant is dormant, the soil should be dry. They like a reasonable amount of humidity and excessively dry air can become a problem for *Glossodia*. Both species in this genus, like many others, have a mycorrhizal relationship with the soil. As a result, a potting mix containing eucalypt shavings or leaf mould is essential to maintain mycorrhiza.

Cultivars

G. major grows to 30 cm tall, bearing 1-2 purple or sometimes white blooms, approximately 4.5 cm across.

G. minor has smaller flowers to 2.5 cm across on stems up to 15 cm tall. Each plant usually produces only a single flower (very rarely two).

These two species hybridise occasionally.

Laelia

(Abbreviation – L.)

Laelia is closely related to *Cattleya*. Consisting of approximately 30 species, and with many varieties in existence, *Laelia* is a genus of epiphytes that are native to Central and South America, predominantly from Brazil. Pseudobulbs each carry 1-2 fleshy leaves that are folded along their length. The flowers have petals that are wider than the sepals. Both petals and sepals are spreading and the lip is variable and can be simple or 3-lobed.

Culture

Cultural treatment does vary according to the species. Some need a definite rest period without watering, while others need to be watered throughout all seasons, as they continue growing all year round.

Ideally the plant will have a winter temperature of 13°C minimum and a summer maximum temperature of around 22°C. Most plants do well grown in open hanging baskets.

Propagate by division in spring.

Cultivars

There are two main groups of *Laelia* that are commonly cultivated.

- Mainly larger flowering plants: these are similar to *Cattleya labiata*. They are a clavate-bulbed species; they do not need a rest in winter.
- Usually smaller flowering plants: these often feature ovoid pseudobulbs. They generally have tall slender flowers that are suitable for growing in warm humid places. They need a good rest over winter.

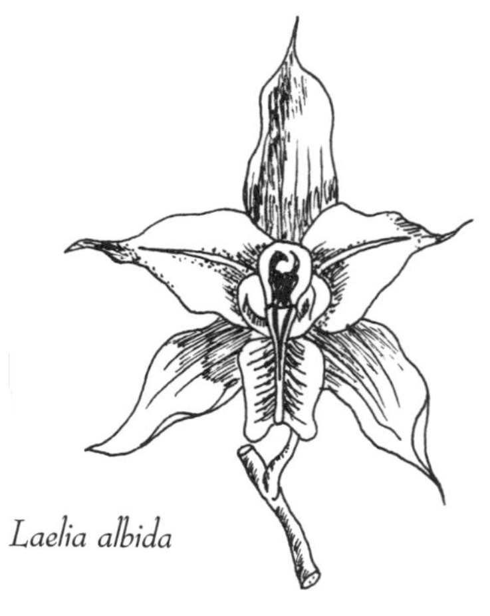

Laelia albida

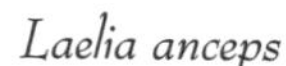

Laelia anceps

L. albida has a short pseudobulb with leaves 17 cm long. Fragrant white flowers are tinged rose and pink. Lip is 3-lobed with yellow crests down the centre.

L. anceps has pseudobulbs to 12 cm long, and leaves to 18 cm long; the flower spikes grow to almost 1 m. It has the largest flowers of all cultivated *Laelia*. Flower characteristics are extremely variable. They can reach 10 cm across, occurring in late autumn or winter, and are commonly pinkish with a yellow-marked and purplish 3-lobed lip in the centre. Other varieties have pale to deep rose flowers with a crimson lip. This species needs a definite rest in winter after flowering, and likes heat and humidity over summer.

L. crispa has pseudobulbs to 30 cm long and leaves to 30 cm. Flower spikes are up to 30 cm long with 4-7 flowers per stem. Flowers occur in summer to early winter, are white and purple, with 3-lobed lips which have purple margins and a yellow throat. *L. crispa* enjoys sun and needs humidity in summer. It must be rested in winter.

L. dormaniana grows to 40 cm tall with thin round stems and 2-4 flowers per spike. Each flower is around 8 cm across, with greenish-brown petals and sepals, and a rose to purplish lip.

L. grandis produces brown-yellow petals and sepals with rose-purple veins. *L. grandis* var. *tenebrosa* has sepals and petals of yellow and a purple trumpet-shaped lip, with a white margin and purple veins.

L. jongheana does not need a rest. Its flowers grow to 12 cm across and are rose to purplish, with yellow markings.

L. lobata has leathery leaves to 10 cm long and flower spikes to 20 cm long with 2-5 flowers per spike. These flowers are rose-purple with deeper-coloured veins, and have a purplish lip. It needs a rest in winter.

L. pumila has pseudobulbs to 10 cm long and leaves to 10 cm. The flower stems grow to 8 cm long bearing a single flower; most commonly the flowers are purplish with yellowish throats, and occur mainly in autumn. Cultivars of *L. pumila* can be variable. It does not require resting (so water all year).

L. purpurata has pseudobulbs to 45 cm long, leaves to 40 cm, and flower spikes to 30 cm. There are 3-7 flowers per spike, often white to rose-flushed with a red-purple lip, and a yellow throat with purple venation. Flowers occur in spring. Flower colour can vary greatly between varieties. *L. purpurata* does not require a rest period.

Hybrids

Many intergeneric hybrids are grown. Crosses with *Cattleya* (called *Laeliocattleya*) in particular are common.

Lycaste

(Abbreviation – Lyc.)

There are approximately 40 species of these deciduous or semi-deciduous, epiphytic orchids. They are native to tropical America. Their pseudobulbs have 1-3 leaves, and the leaves have a petiole. Flower stems bear a single flower which is most often greenish, but the colours vary a lot. The flowers have a waxy appearance and are long lasting.

Culture

Grow *Lycaste* in medium shade to prevent burning, but avoid heavy shade. Deciduous species prefer 50-70% shade; evergreen or semi-deciduous species like more. Plants prefer warm conditions with a minimum temperature of 15°C or above, although some will tolerate cooler minimums. In winter minimum night temperatures may be around 10°C, ranging in summer up to around 19°C.

Avoid wetting the plants' foliage. Never allow the roots to become too wet, but they should be kept moist during growth periods (normally water more in summer). Immediately after flowering the roots should be allowed to dry out for a couple of weeks. Deciduous species should remain dry while they are leafless.

During active growth the ideal humidity is 40-70%, but keep it low for deciduous species during dormancy. Ventilation is important: still air combined with pools of water around pots can easily lead to disease.

Fertilise regularly when the plants are actively growing, but reduce feeding as foliage matures and pseudobulbs form.

These orchids like a potting medium similar to that used for cymbidiums. A good mix might be three parts pine bark to one part perlite. Place crocks or chunky material in the base of the pot to facilitate drainage and aeration.

Propagate by division of large plants, or by removing and planting single healthy back bulbs in a chunky orchid medium and laying moist sphagnum moss on its surface.

Cultivars

L. aromatica has pseudobulbs 8-10 cm long, which carry green leaves to 50 cm long. Flowers are yellow and very fragrant, and normally occur in spring.

L. Deppei (syn. *Maxillaria deppei*) has ovoid pseudobulbs 5-10 cm long, each with several leaves to 50 cm in length. Flowers, which occur in summer or early autumn, grow to 6 cm long. They have pale green, red-flecked sepals, white petals with red flecks, and a yellow lip with red markings. *L. Deppei* is easy to grow and tolerates temperatures to 8°C.

L. skinneri (syn. *L. virginalis*) is a particularly popular plant, but is a challenge to grow. Pseudobulbs are around 10 cm long, each with several leaves to 60 cm. Flower stems grow to 15 cm long with flowers up to 15 cm across. These vary in form and colour: a white form is the national flower of Guatemala.

L. xytriophora has a compact growing habit with greenish-brown sepals and yellow-green to white petals.

Hybrids

Angulocaste: parents are from *Lycaste* and the genus *Anguloa*.

Zygocaste: parents are from *Lycaste* and *Zygopetalum*.

These hybrids are treated in the same way as *Lycaste*.

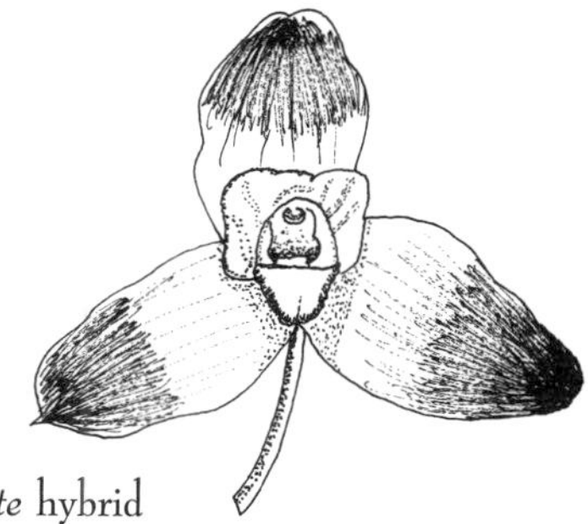

Lycaste hybrid

MASDEVALLIA

(Abbreviation – Masd.)

These orchids include approximately 300 species of epiphytes from the highlands of tropical America. They have short stems (no pseudobulbs) with a single, normally leathery, leaf. Flowers are terminal, and can be multiple or borne singly; they occur mainly in spring. Sepals are joined to some extent at the base into a tube or cup, the petals are smaller and narrow, and the lip is small.

Culture

Provide 70% shade in temperate areas (e.g. Tasmania and Victoria) during the worst of the summer, and even more shade in warmer areas. However, excessive shade can be just as detrimental as too little.

If the centre of new growth is allowed to remain moist it can easily rot during warm conditions. Over summer try to maintain good ventilation around plants, and keep maximum temperatures from exceeding 25-30°C. Root level temperatures should not exceed 20°C.

Water on a daily basis during the hottest weather, but be cautious of moss or algae becoming too thick on pots: remove them if this happens as they can stop water from penetrating.

A weak fertiliser added to daily waterings may be better than using slow release fertilisers like Osmocote.

Slugs and snails are a particular problem as they attack the flowers, so use snail baits liberally, being careful as always to protect small children or pets.

Propagate by division in mid-summer. Take 6-10 leaves per division.

Cultivars

M. chimaera has narrow leaves to 13 cm long; flower stems are up to 18 cm tall, and flower parts are primarily yellow with additional colourations. There are various named cultivars of this species.

M. coccinea has flowers which vary in size and colour, but are most frequently magenta-scarlet to purple. The flower stalk grows up to 30 cm tall.

M. glandulosa has elliptical-shaped leaves growing to about 13 cm long and 2 cm wide, and with a distinct leaf stalk. Flower stems grow to around 10 cm tall, each with a single purplish flower, which occurs in winter.

M. ignea (syn. *M. militaris*) produces upright glossy leaves to 25 cm, or less, which have a distinct leaf stalk. Reddish to purple or orange flowers occur in late spring or autumn.

M. infracta produces delicate sulphur-coloured flowers borne in succession.

M. macrura is a robust plant with leathery leaves to around 30 cm long, with large brownish to yellow flowers with black to purplish markings.

M. maculata grows to 13 cm tall, and bears yellow flowers with purple markings.

M. polysticta has purple-spotted flowers up to 6 cm across.

M. racemosa has flower stems up to 38 cm long, which hold 8-15 orange-red flowers shaded with crimson. The leaves grow to around 10 cm long.

M. triangularis has leaves to around 15 cm long, and yellow to greenish summer flowers with a dense covering of brownish spots.

M. Veitchiana has leaves to around 20 cm long, and large brilliant orange-red flowers up to 6 cm wide, borne on stalks 45 cm long.

MAXILLARIA

(Abbreviation – Max.)

There are 300-350 species of *Maxillaria*. Classification is often confusing, and some authorities quote more than 350 species. At one time there were up to 700 species, before several related plants were identified as separate genera. These now include *Camaridium*, *Dicrypta*, *Lycaste*, *Menadenia*, *Ornithidium*, *Pentulops* and *Xylobium*. Most come from tropical South America, some from Central America, the Carribean, and even Florida.

Maxillaria are small or large, mostly epiphytes (though some may be lithophytes or terrestrial). Stems can become pseudobulbs, or be stem-like, completely lacking pseudobulbs. When present, pseudobulbs each have one to (rarely) four narrow leaves. They can have single or many flowers, and the flowers can be small or large. Growth habits vary also: some spread across the ground, some are climbing, while others have more clumping habits.

Culture

Most like plenty of light (but never direct sun), good ventilation and high humidity.

Most species are rested (i.e. allowed to dry out) for a period in winter, but the duration of that rest can vary greatly. Species with harder bulbs and harder more robust foliage need a more definite rest. Species with more tender foliage, and strongly keeled leaves, are rested for no more than a week or two (e.g. *M. Sanderana*).

Some species originate in cooler places, in which case they may tolerate lower temperatures, while others come from hotter climates, and should always be kept warm.

Propagation is usually by division in spring.

The environmental origin of the orchid is the best indicator of cultivation requirements.

Cultivars

M. chrysantha is a vigorous species with yellow flowers, and grows well under medium temperatures in a greenhouse or shadehouse.

M. desvauxiana has pinkish flowers flushed with red and yellow, borne from the base of the pseudobulb.

M. juergensis has deep red spotted flowers.

M. marginata has yellow to orange flowers with red edging. It has a rambling growth habit.

M. picta has pear-shaped pseudobulbs and fragrant flowers. Petals and sepals are brown-green to yellow inside, and white with dark spots on the outer surface.

M. porphyrostele produces masses of yellow flowers in spring. It has good cold- and drought-tolerance.

M. rufescens has scented yellow to darkened orange flowers with red spots.

M. Sanderana is considered one of the most attractive species. It produces a cluster of pseudobulbs, each carrying one thick leaf to around 40 cm long, and whitish flowers with purple and yellow markings.

M. triloris is a large-growing orchid with up to six scented flowers per pseudobulb. Flowers are primarily white, suffused with red on the outside and yellow on the inside.

Maxillaria venusta

M. venusta is a tight-growing orchid with strappy foliage and white flowers with a yellow and maroon flushed lip.

MILTONIA (PANSY ORCHID)

(Abbreviation – Milt.)

Miltonia is closely related to *Miltoniopsis*, *Odontoglossum* and *Oncidium*. There are approximately 25 species, all epiphytes and native to the highlands of tropical and South America; most are from the highlands of Brazil. Their pseudobulbs generally have only two leaves with a sheath at their base. Flowers are axillary, basal, loosely racemose, and there can be one or several flowers per stem.

Culture

Some species grow at minimum temperatures as low as 6°C, but many prefer minimums of 12°C or more. For most, summer maximums of around 27°C are suitable.

Most Brazilian species prefer to grow on slabs.

Water generously and fertilise when the plant is actively growing; preferably apply both water and fertiliser to the back of a slab or through capillary watering (e.g. sitting the plant in a dish of weak liquid fertiliser). This way you minimise wetting the foliage, which encourages rotting. Reduce watering by about a third after the growth period, but never let the plants totally dry out.

Remount on a slab or repot into an open slab basket every two years; this is best carried out on a cool day, after new growth commences.

Miltonia generally tolerate more diverse conditions than *Miltoniopsis*.

Cultivars

M. candida produces small numbers of large (to 8 cm across) chestnut-brown flowers with yellow markings. The lip is white with a reddish tinge at the base. Another cultivar of this species (*M. candida* 'Grandiflora') has flowers twice as large and more brown in colour.

M. favescens has elliptical to oblong flattened pseudobulbs up to 15 cm long. Leaves are linear strap-like and to 30 cm in length. Flowers occur in summer, with long thin pale yellow-green petals and sepals, and a large white lip with purplish streaks.

M. Regnellii has ovate to oblong pseudobulbs to 8 cm long, and linear strap-like leaves to 30 cm long. Flowers are up to 8 cm across with white petals flushed with pink. The lip has rose, purple and yellow colourings. There are 3-5 flowers on a spike which is taller than the leaves.

M. Roezlii has 2-6 fragrant flowers on a spike, usually predominantly white, but with some markings.

M. spectabilis has flattened ovate to oblong pseudobulbs at short intervals on a rhizome, and linear strap-like leaves to 15 cm long. Flowers appear in summer or autumn, and are large fragrant and cream-white with yellow and rose-coloured markings. There can be up to 250 flowers on a single flower spike.

M. vexillaria has up to eight light green leaves emerging from each pseudobulb. Normally two flower spikes grow from a bulb, each weeping and to 50 cm long. Each spike carries 4-7 large flowers to 10 cm across. Flower size and colour can vary, and there are several named varieties in cultivation.

M. Jersey has attractive large white blooms with bold red markings and a yellow throat.

Hybrids

Most *Miltonia* hybrids are called 'tropical Miltonias' and are bred from Brazilian varieties of *M. spectabilis*, *M. Regnellii*, or *Miltoniopsis Warcewiczii* or similar species. In contrast to *Miltoniopsis* hybrids, *Miltonia* hybrids have a spreading growth habit, and their leaves are generally a traditional green colour. Flower colours vary from dark reds to almost white.

Miltonioda, a hybrid between *Miltonia* and *Cochlioda*, and *Miltonidium* hybrids between *Oncidium* and *Miltonia*, have small-sized but richly coloured flowers and prefer warm temperatures, like *Oncidium*.

Miltonioides is a new closely related genus made up of species previously included under *Oncidium*, *Miltonia* and other genera. These generally like conditions a little drier than *Miltonia* or *Odontoglossum*.

Miltonia have also been extensively hybridised with *Odontoglossum* and *Brassia*.

The differences between *Miltonia* and *Miltoniopsis* are:
- *Miltoniopsis* has more exaggerated labella than *Miltonia*.
- *Miltoniopsis* generally has softer foliage and is more prone to disease and die-back than *Miltonia*.
- *Miltoniopsis* has one leaf per pseudobulb, while *Miltonia* has two.

MILTONIOPSIS

(Abbreviation – Milt.)

(Note: The official abbreviation is a little confusing because many authorities consider this genus to be actually a *Miltonia*: the same abbreviation as *Miltonia* is used in this book. Some authorities do not allocate any abbreviation to *Miltoniopsis*.)

Originally classified under *Miltonia*, *Miltoniopsis* is still considered by many authorities to belong within that genus. These orchids are cool-growing, coming mainly from altitudes between 1300 and 1250 m in Columbia. The pseudobulbs have one leaf.

A healthy *Miltoniopsis* in full flower is one of the most attractive of all orchids.

Culture

For good performance keep temperatures between 15° and 28°C. A minimum of 13°C is preferred.

Miltoniopsis DO NOT have a dormancy period, so keep their medium moist all year. Fertilise with weak nutrients regularly, perhaps fortnightly, when they are growing most, and monthly when growth slows.

Miltoniopsis Warscewiczii

They are less hardy, and require more water than *Miltonia*. They also need constant air flow, so fans are often used in greenhouses where these orchids are grown.

Grow them in a relatively fine (not chunky) potting medium (e.g. 2 mm-diameter composted bark and aggregate). If they are potted into too large a pot they may become excessively moist and their roots may rot. If the plant is healthy, the roots are vigorous; if not, remove old potting medium, treat any diseases or pests, then repot in a mix of sphagnum and terracotta crocks. Keep this always moist, but not wet, and the plant should be reinvigorated within three months.

Forcing flowers to come at the wrong time can make them more susceptible to disease. Flowers last up to three weeks on the plants, but deteriorate quickly if taken as cut flowers.

Cultivars

M. Warcewiczii has flattened oblong pseudobulbs to 13 cm long, and linear to oblong leaves to 18 cm in length. There is one leaf per pseudobulb. Flower spikes are up to 35 cm long with many flowers. The flowers are red to brown and tipped with yellow, the lip is rose-purple with white and brown markings, and occur in late winter or early spring.

Hybrids

Most hybrids are compact (not spreading), the pseudobulbs and foliage are pale blue to green, and the arching flower spikes are normally reddish to shades of yellow or white.

M. Beall's Strawberry Joy has pale pink and white blooms with a deep red splash near the throat.

Odontoglossum

(Abbreviation – Odm.)

Related to *Oncidium* and *Miltonia*, this is a large and variable genus with many hybrids and approximately 250 species of epiphytes or lithophytes. *Odontoglossum* are native to the cool mountains of tropical America.

They generally have flattened pseudobulbs, and their leaves have a fold along their length.

The inflorescence is racemose, or paniculate and lateral. Flowers can be small or large, few or many, and are often showy and long-lasting. Sepals and petals are spreading and similar, while the lip often has a distinctive claw parallel to the column.

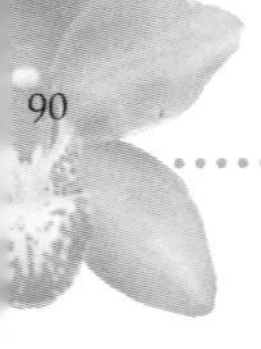

Culture

For good growth *Odontoglossum* need day temperatures that don't fall below 15°C, but preferably mild conditions rather than hot. Night temperatures should rarely go below 12°C. Avoid cold draughts, but in cool climates some fresh air is necessary if the plants are grown indoors. Some like cooler conditions than others (e.g. *O. crispum* is better suited to cooler positions).

Like *Cattleya*, *Odontoglossum* prefer good sunlight, but not direct sun. They will require more shade if temperatures are high. Constant high humidity is necessary, ideally around 70% and never below 40%. Misting may be used (morning only) to raise humidity in drier climates. Dampening the floor of a greenhouse or fogging might also be used to raise humidity. Good ventilation is also important, so use fans if you need to.

Fertilise twice a month when growth is active, but reduce to once monthly if the light level is lower (e.g. overcast weather). Use less nitrogen in fertiliser if your plants are on slabs, or in a non-bark medium; use more potassium and phosphorus as flowering draws close.

Repot when new growth starts, perhaps every two years, usually in spring or autumn. After potting, keep humidity high and the pot drier until new roots are moving.

When the plant is overgrown in the pot, you can propagate by partly cutting the rhizome attached to the pseudobulb and leaving it until new growth begins on it; or you can completely sever the pseudobulb immediately and plant it separately from the rest of the plant. Transplant or divide in autumn or early spring, never in hot summer weather. Do not over-pot: plants do much better when confined or crowded.

Cultivars

O. cirrhosum has flattened pseudostems with 1-2 leaves. Flowers are borne on arching racemes; they are white, spotted with maroon-crimson.

O. crispum has flattened pseudobulbs with linear leaves to 30 cm long. Drooping stems carry many flowers, each around 8 cm across; they are commonly white with rose-violet markings; however, there are many named varieties. The plants prefer maximum day temperatures of around 22°C.

O. grande (Tiger Orchid) (syn. *Rossioglossum grande*) has narrow leaves to 30-40 cm long; pseudobulbs each carry 2-3 leaves. Relatively few but large flowers (to 15 cm across) are borne on an upright stem. They are bright yellow with brownish markings, and a fringed lip. The plants require similar temperatures to *Cattleya*.

O. Harryanum has leathery leaves to 25 cm long; relatively few showy flowers, to 9 cm across, are borne on an erect raceme; the lip has fringed margins. The plants require similar temperature to *Cymbidium*.

Odontoglossum cirrhosum

O. luteopurpureum carries large, ovoid pseudobulbs and the leaves grow to 60 cm. The flower spike is long and either semi-upright or arching, and carries lots of showy flowers, each to around 10 cm across. This species prefers maximum day temperatures of around 22°C. There are several named varieties which provide flower variations.

O. pendulum (syn. *Cuitlauzina pendula*) has ovoid to globe-shaped pseudobulbs and oblong, strap-like leaves to 30 cm long. Pendulous sprays contain many fragrant flowers, each around 7 cm across or more. Flowers tend to be white to rose in colour and occur in late spring. This species has similar temperature requirements to Cattleyas, but prefers slightly more shade.

O. pulchellum (Lily of the Valley Orchid) has leaves and flower spikes both approximately 40 cm long. The flower spikes contain many showy, predominantly white, flowers; the lip is yellow with red dots. It needs similar temperatures to *Cattleya*, but slightly more shade.

O. Rossii has fleshy leaves to 10 cm long. Showy flowers occur in winter and are commonly yellow to greenish with red to brown spots. There are usually one to several (not many) on an erect 15-20 cm spike, each around 7 cm across. *O. Rossii* requires a similar temperature to *Cymbidium*.

Hybrids

Various natural and artificially raised hybrids are grown.

Odm. Castro × *Torpesca* has frilled petals and sepals with a mottled pink pattern. The throat remains sulphur yellow in colour.

Odontioda results from crosses with *Cochlioda* and *Odontoglossum*, which have created some brilliant flower colours.

Odontobrassia is from a cross between *Odontoglossum* and *Brassia*. They have relatively large flowers with the spider-like shape of *Brassia*.

ONCIDIUM (DANCING LADY ORCHID)

(Abbreviation – Onc.)

There are approximately 400 species of *Oncidium*, originating in both the cool mountains and hot lowlands of tropical America. They are epiphytes, and most usually produce well-developed pseudobulbs. Leaves are flat and thick, occurring either singly or overlapping in two ranks. The flower stalk can hold few or many large or small flowers.

Culture

Oncidium need lots of light, some species like almost, but not entirely, direct sun; others may prefer 40-60% shade in summer.

They are mainly tropical plants requiring high humidity and, for most, temperatures preferably no lower than 13°C. If humidity and air movement levels are high they will tolerate temperatures of 35°C or above. The hardiest varieties require a similar climate to the average *Cattleya*.

Generally watering should be reduced over winter; in fact many species grow naturally in areas that receive no rainfall at all for more than six months of the year. Though pseudobulbs can shrivel up over the dry season, they still regrow into healthy plants come the wet season. Humidity is best kept at 30-60% which is not normally a problem in a greenhouse. Misting might be needed if the plants are growing in a dry hot climate. Good aeration is important.

Fertilise every two weeks when the plants are in active growth; if weather becomes overcast reduce this frequency.

Oncidium are grown either as epiphytes on slabs of tree fern or wood, or in a very coarse open potting mix, coarser than for *Cymbidium*. An ideal potting mix can be made from chunky pine bark mixed with 5-10 mm diameter non-porous stone (e.g. blue metal – avoid scoria as it is very porous).

Normally repot in spring when new growth starts from the base.

Cultivars

There are two types of *Oncidium*: Climbing Types, grown as a climbing rhizome, and Spreading Types, grown as creeping rhizomes.

The most commonly grown varieties are hybrids of either *O. crispum*, *O. varicosum* or one or two other species.

O. cebolleta (syn. *O. longifolium*) is a free-blooming species from tropical America, which has been cultivated for almost 200 years. Though not the best *Oncidium*, it produces many attractive, mainly yellow, flowers with reddish spots. Size is extremely variable.

O. clowessii has a large lip, purplish in the centre and paler at the tip. The petals and sepals are strikingly yellow with brownish markings.

O. crispum has leaves to around 25 cm long, and can produce large numbers of variable flowers, often with chestnut-brown and yellow colourings.

O. flexuosum is a free-flowering, greatly branched plant with dainty yellow flowers. It can, however, be temperamental in cultivation.

O. ornithororhynchum is more cold-tolerant than some species. It has fragrant, pink flowers with a yellowish centre.

O. sphacelatum has long thick leaves to 70 cm, and rich yellow to orange flowers with brown-red markings.

O. varicosum has light green strap leaves to 25 cm long. The very large flower spikes can reach up to 1.5 m in length, carrying large numbers of mainly yellow flowers. This species is better adapted to mild climates than most others.

Hybrids

Oncidium have been extensively hybridised, some plants with only *Oncidium* parents, and others which share parentage with other genera.

Onc. Golden Shower, bred from *O. flexuosum* × *O. sphacelatum* in Singapore, is sold widely as a cut flower from South East Asia. It has bold yellow flowers.

Onc. Golden Sunset × Onc. Trixie Richella is predominately butter yellow in colour with orange-brown markings.

Onc. Sharry Baby is a cultivar with deep red, scented flowers produced in profusion.

Howeara is a hybrid from *Oncidium* × *Leochilis* × *Rodriguesia*.

Odontocidium are hybrids created by breeding *Odontoglossum* with *Oncidium*.

These generally have good-sized flowers on large sprays.

Odontocidium Tiger Hambuien is a hybrid that produces attractive white flowers with dull red markings that look as though they have been painted onto the petals.

Wilsonaria results from *Oncidium* × *Odontoglossum* × *Cochlioda*.

PAPHIOPEDILUM (SLIPPER ORCHIDS OR LADY'S SLIPPER)

(Abbreviation – Paph.)

Paphiopedilum belong to a relatively primitive group of orchids that also includes the genera *Phragmipedium* and *Cypripedium*. All of these genera have the lip shaped like the toe of a slipper or a pouch: hence they are commonly known as Lady's Slippers.

There are approximately 60 species of *Paphiopedilum*. They are terrestrial or epiphytic plants from tropical Asia. They have leathery leaves folded along their length, which emerge from the base of the plant. The leaves can sometimes have a mottled colouration. Flowers can be solitary or in a raceme. The dorsal sepal is usually larger; lateral ones are always united. The lip is slipper- or pouch-shaped. Some species do not flower readily; others flower more easily.

Culture

Reduce watering over winter, and water only when the top of the pot is becoming dry. However, increase watering during warmer months, and protect the plants from strong drying winds. Aeration is particularly important; shallow pots are normally preferred and are best placed on a wire mesh bench, or something off the ground, to allow air movement around the base of the pot.

Repot annually in spring. Well-developed plants can be divided just before active growth begins.

Scale and mealy bug are often a problem over summer.

As well as consistent watering over summer, apply soluble fertiliser regularly. Avoid high temperatures (over 30°C) by shading, misting and/or ventilation; never allow temperatures to reach below 12-14°C.

One of the easiest slipper orchids to grow is *P. insigne*, which flowers in autumn and has even been grown on an indoor windowsill in a mild climate such as Sydney.

A good *Paphiopedilum* potting mix is a little richer and heavier than most other tropical orchid mixes (e.g. 80% of 5-10 mm diameter pine bark, 18% of 5-10 mm diameter charcoal, 2% shell grit, and a pinch of blood and bone per pot). Always wet the potting mix thoroughly before using.

These orchids flower mainly over winter. Flower quality is affected by several things including watering, feeding, staking and light.

Reduce shading considerably from mid-autumn to mid-spring. Do not water at this time unless reasonably dry, and on a sunny day water only in the early morning.

Cultivars

There are two broad types of *Paphiopedilum*:

- Species that occur naturally at high altitudes in cool moist conditions. These tend to have green, grass-like leaves, and to flower in winter. They prefer 10-13°C at night, and a maximum of around 21°C . Without low night temperatures for a few months at least, they will not flower. It is important to keep summer maximums low for these species.

- Species that occur in warm forests, close to the ground. These tend to have mottled foliage; they usually flower in summer but some can flower at any time of the year. These orchids need night minimums of around 15-20°C and day maximums of 21-30°C. These will tolerate more heat than species from the other group.

Hybrids derived from crosses of these two types commonly prefer conditions between the two. Hybrids are often relatively easy to grow, so much so that they are sometimes called a 'beginner's orchid'.

P. barbatum has mottled, leathery leaves. The scape (flower stem) is long, dark purple in colour, and lightly hairy. Flowers can reach 10 cm across. The sepals are white with a pale green base, the petals greenish near the base, changing to purple towards the top and with blackish markings; the lip is purplish brown. Flowers occur from winter to late summer.

P. bellatulum has leaves mottled on the upper surface, and purplish beneath. The scape is shorter than the leaves. Flowers can reach 8 cm across, and are white to creamy yellow, with purple-brown spots. *P. bellatulum* will grow on limestone rock. It is free flowering, but can be difficult to cultivate. It must be protected from rain.

P. callosum has mottled blackish-green leaves, and a long scape with 1-2 flowers to 10 cm across. Sepals are white with purplish and green veins, petals are greenish lower down, changing to rose at the tip, with blackish markings; the lip is helmet-shaped, with purplish colouration. Flowering is in late winter.

P. concolor has mottled leaves, greyish to green on the upper surface, and spotted with crimson on the lower. The scape is shorter than the leaves and carries one or two pale yellow flowers with purplish markings, each to 5 cm across.

P. glaucophyllum has greyish-green leaves to 23 cm long. Up to 21 flowers are carried on an erect greenish-brown hairy scape to 45 cm high. Sepals are yellowish-green with a yellowish margin, petals white with reddish or purple blotches, and the lip is rose-purple with darker blotches and a light green edge. This orchid comes from east Java, and is one of the most free flowering species of *Paphiopedilum*.

P. *hirsutissimum* has green leaves to 30 cm. The flower scape has fine purple hairs. Flowers are up to 10 cm across. Dark purple-red spots appear in all flower parts for a striking effect.

P. insigne has green leaves to 30 cm long. The purplish flower scape is generally shorter than the leaves, lightly hairy, and carries only 1-2 flowers. There is great variation in flower characteristics with many named varieties. This species is perhaps the most commonly cultivated, and is relatively easy to grow.

P. Lawrenceanum has mottled leaves. The scape is longer than the leaves, is purplish-brown in colour, and carries only 1-2 flowers, each to 13 cm across. Sepals are white with green to purplish veins, and petals are greenish, changing to purple near the tips and with 5-10 black markings on each margin. The lip is purplish to brown above, and greenish below. Flowering is in spring to summer.

P. rothschildianum has leaves to 90 cm long. The sepals are whitish with prominent dark stripes; the thinner petals are speckled and the reddish-violet lip is yellow on top.

Hybrids

While many species come from tropical areas, most hybrids are more suited to cooler conditions than the extreme humid tropics. In South East Asia, most hybrids grow better in cooler mountain areas than the hotter lowlands.

P. Milmanii is produced from *P. philippinense* × *P. callosum* in Singapore, and is a good strong flowering plant.

Phaius

This genus is closely related to *Calanthe*.

There are approximately 50 species of these terrestrial orchids. Mature plants are frequently bulky with a mass of pseudobulbs. Most are native to Australia, South East Asia, and into China. Some come from India and Madagascar.

Foliage can vary; some have short stems, while others produce pseudobulbs or slender leafy plants. The leaves are commonly large, usually thinly textured, but with obvious veins.

Flowers can occur singly or in clusters, and are more often large, tall and showy, arising from the base on upright stems, sometimes up to 2 m tall. The lip is usually large and wide.

Culture

Depending on the species, good winter minimums are 13°C (for hardier types) to 20°C (for more tropical types). Summer maximums in the shade should be around 27°C.

The plants usually need a good level of humidity when in active growth, but be careful about moisture (particularly water on the foliage) when the plants are dormant or growth is slow. They generally need only light shade.

Apply weak fertiliser occasionally while watering when plants are in the growth phase. Reduce watering in winter.

Propagate by dividing a healthy clump, or from a single back bulb if it is particularly large and healthy.

Cultivars

P. australis has dark green pleated leaves up to 1.2 m long. The flower stalk grows up to 2 m tall, carrying 4-16 reddish brown to white flowers, each 10 cm across. This species is native to the mid-east coast of Australia.

P. bernaysii has large leaves to 1.25 m long. The flower stalk grows to 2 m, and bears 4-16 white to yellow flowers, each 10 cm across.

P. flavus (syn. *P. maculatus*) develops a conical pseudostem with 5-8 leaves. The flowers are light yellow with tan markings.

P. humblotii has broad leaves to 50 cm long, and 7-10 flowers on a scape. The flowers are up to 5 cm across and are rose to purple suffused with white.

P. pictus has leaves to 70 cm long. The flower stalk is up to 90 cm long, bearing 4-20 flowers, 5 cm across, and brick-red with a yellow stripe.

P. tankervilliae (syn. *P. grandiflora*) is a swamp orchid, widespread throughout sub-tropical countries, and from the Himalayas. It has variable characteristics (depending on where it comes from). Some types have been given different species names. This is one of the few orchids that will grow with wet feet.

P. tuberculosus has broad leaves 35 cm long; there are up to seven white flowers on a spike, and these are 6 cm across.

Hybrids

Hybrids have been made between *Phaius* and *Calanthe*.

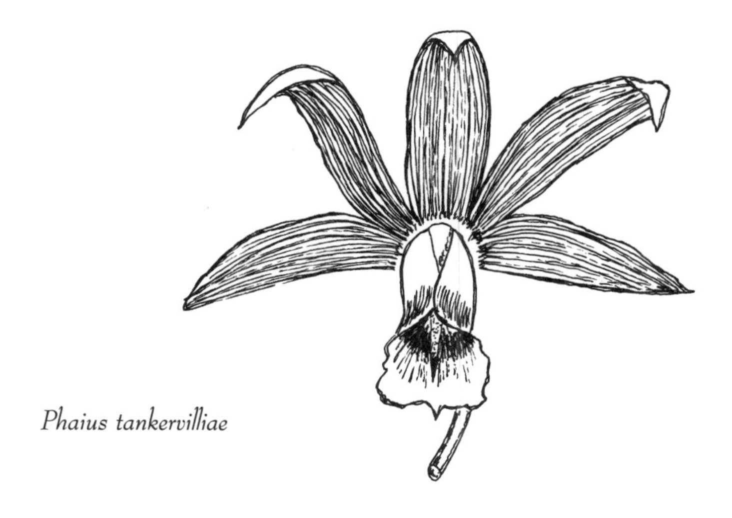

Phaius tankervilliae

Phalaenopsis (MOTH ORCHIDS)

(Abbreviation – Phal.)

These orchids are closely related to *Vanda*. There are approximately 55 species plus thousands of named hybrids of *Phalaenopsis*. They include both epiphytes or lithophytes, and are sometimes deciduous.

Their stems are short and they do NOT have pseudobulbs. The leaves are fleshy and ranked in pairs. They rarely have petioles, and can sometimes be bract-like. The colour and size of the flowers can be variable, according to the variety. The lip is 3-lobed, and usually smaller and more brightly coloured than other parts of the flower.

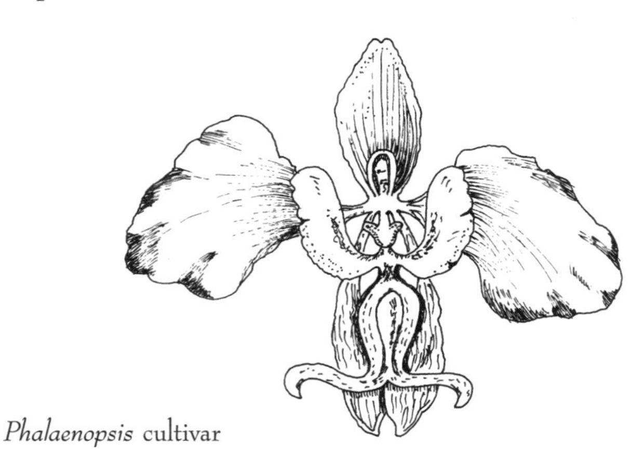

Phalaenopsis cultivar

Culture

In winter, water only early in the morning (maybe every 3-5 days); do not allow the crown to be moist overnight – this can encourage rot. Never water on cold or overcast days in winter.

The plants need a relatively constant environment all year round, with temperatures never below 18°C and rarely above 30°C. They require up to 90% shade over summer in warmer parts of Australia if temperatures ever go above 30°C. Young tender leaves in particular need shading. Reduce the level of shade to 70% in winter. In mild or cool climates, greenhouse-grown *Phalaenopsis* need 70-80% shade in sunny weather (i.e. they need twice the shade of *Cattleya*!).

Plants are commonly grown on weathered pieces of wood or cork, or on fern slabs. They can also be grown in hanging baskets or in shallow pots filled with a very open chunky mix of bark and charcoal. Potting up or mounting should always be finished before summer. Avoid pots that are too large as this can deter good root growth.

Decaying vegetation (e.g. small amounts of leaf mould) are the best food for *Phalaenopsis*. Weak solutions of fish emulsion or seaweed fertiliser are also useful. Never apply fertiliser to dry plants; always water the plants first. Over autumn use fertilisers low in nitrogen and high in potash. Water quality affects performance significantly. Alkaline or saline water will slow growth: pure clean rainwater is best if you care to collect it.

Aphis, mealy bug, scale, mites and fungal diseases are the most likely problems. Routine sprays of fungicide (e.g. Daconil or Mancozeb with Kocide) are often necessary, particularly if you are growing these orchids outside the tropics.

Cultivars

Both hybrids and species are grown widely. There are more than 40,000 named hybrid *Phalaenopsis*, often grouped according to colour: white, pinks, candy stripes, yellows, semi-albas, sandy pinks or novelties.

Species are often grown to use in hybridising new varieties.

There are several named cultivars of *P. amabilis* grown. They have glossy dark green leaves to around 25 cm long. The flowers are fragrant, generally white with yellow in the central lip, and occur in autumn and winter.

P. amboinensis has leaves to around 25 cm long, and a flower spike to 45 cm, producing a succession of small numbers of flowers. These have pale yellowish petals and sepals with large reddish-brown markings.

P. Aphrodite (the Taiwan Butterfly Orchid) is sometimes confused with *P. amabilis*. The flowers are white to occasionally pinkish, and the lip differs from *P. amabilis*.

P. equestris has fleshy bright green leaves to 20 cm long; the pale pink flowers have a darker pink lip and a yellow or white crest.

P. Lindenii has silvery-white mottled green leaves. The flowers are white to pale pink with rose dots; the column is usually purple.

P. Mariae has broad glossy green leaves; the flowers have pale petals, whitish to cream, and sepals covered with large brownish patches.

P. violacea has fragrant flowers, commonly pale greenish-white at the edges, changing to dark purplish-pink in the centre. There are cultivars with quite a few variations in flower colour.

Hybrids

There are many thousands of *Phalaenopsis* hybrids in cultivation, including both those bred within the genus, and others bred with other related genera. The first white hybrid was *P. Elisabethae* (*P. amabilis* × *P. rimestadiana*). Today we know these two parents as being varieties of the same species. Nevertheless, since being registered in 1927, *P. Elisabethae* has become the parent of a very large number of popular modern hybrids.

P. sanderiana and *P. schilleriana* have also been used extensively in hybridisation:

- *Phal*. Ho's Queen Brother has large white flowers with distinct red dots throughout the petals and sepals.
- *Phal*. Elegant Dame produces large flowers suffused with pink.

Hybrids produced by breeding with other genera include:

- *Aeridopsis – Aerides* × *Phalaenopsis*
- *Arachnopsis – Arachnis* × *Phalaenopsis*
- *Asconopsis – Ascocenda* × *Phalaenopsis*
- *Doritaenopsis – Doritis* × *Phalaenopsis*
- *Renanthopsis – Renanthera* × *Phalaenopsis*
- *Vandaenopsis – Vanda* × *Phalaenopsis*
- *Vandopsis – Phalandopsis* × *Phalaenopsis*.

PHRAGMIPEDIUM (MANDARIN ORCHIDS)

(Abbreviation – Phrag.)

There are around 20 species of *Phragmipedium* from Mexico and South America. They are closely related to *Paphiopedilum*.

Phragmipedium occur naturally on rocks, in forks of trees and in volcanic clay soils. They flower mostly in spring, but can produce flowers up to 11 months of the year. They have very large flowers with long ribbon petals: these can be over 70 cm long. Flower colours are variable, including shades of green to pink to orange. Foliage is similar to green-leaved *Paphiopedilum*.

Culture

The plants prefer bright light (but avoid extremes that will burn foliage). Most take a little more light than *Phalaenopsis* or *Paphiopedilum*, but some species have different light requirements: for most 60-75% shade or up to 80% in bright conditions is appropriate.

Water is best slightly acidic (pH 5.5 or lower) though many species will tolerate pH to slightly above neutral. Water cleanliness can also be important for some, so if possible avoid muddy water.

Humidity at a level of 50-70% is preferable.

Fertilise every 2-3 weeks in spring and summer with weak fertiliser; reduce to half as often in winter. These plants are easily burnt with excessive feeding. A sprinkling of blood and bone may be better.

Bacterial rot at the base of the leaves can be a problem in summer. Any potting mix must drain fast (chunky bark and charcoal with some sphagnum moss is good), but keep the medium always moist. Generally, repot only if the potting medium begins to decompose. If the plant is grown in a bark mix, repot every two years. Many species also grow well in rockwool (rockwool-grown plants need to be flushed with clean water at least monthly to wash away any salt build-up).

Propagate by division; you will need 3-4 growths at least for flowering, so do not make divisions smaller than this.

Cultivars

P. Boisserianum has strap-shaped leaves to 50 cm long; a flower spike (raceme) to 50 cm long bears 3-10 flowers. The flowers are large, yellowish-green with dark green venation. The petals have white or brown borders. The plants grow naturally in volcanic clay.

P. calurum has pale rose flowers with deeper rose colouring to the dorsal side. Growth habit and appearance is similar to other *Phragmipedium* orchids.

P. caudatum is a terrestrial that can also grow in the fork of a tree. The flowers are yellowish with long robust ribbon-like petals which hang and twist. It tolerates drier conditions than some species, likes levels of light similar to *Cattleya*, and tolerates lower humidity than other *Phragmepidum* species.

P. longifolium has leaves to 60 cm long; the flower spikes grow to 1 m and bear more flowers than many other *Phagmipedium* often do. Flowers are greenish with bronze to red markings.

P. pearcei has pointed linear leaves to 50 cm long. The upright flower spike bears large long-lasting attractive flowers, predominantly green, white and purplish.

P. Schlimii has strap-shaped leaves to 30 cm in length; the flower spike is longer than the leaves but has only a few flowers, each to 5 cm across. The petals are oval-shaped (not long and thin like other *Phragmipedium*), and can be white or pinkish to darker rose. The lip can be rose-carmine to yellow.

P. wallisii grows in volcanic clay and tolerates drier conditions than some species.

Hybrids

Several hybrids are cultivated, including *Phrag.* × *Sedenii*. This is a hybrid of *P. longifolium* × *P. Schlimii*. It has two pale sepals, two darker and thinner pink to purplish petals, and a yellow-greenish lip. It has been known to grow submerged in water during heavy rainfall.

Pleione (INDIAN CROCUS, NEPALESE ORCHIDS, WINDOWSILL ORCHIDS)

(Abbreviation – Pln.)

There are around 10 species (some authorities say up to 15) of *Pleione*, all terrestrial plants and mainly from mild Asian climates. The pseudobulbs are corm-like. Each pseudobulb produces either one or two leaves only.

They usually produce only single but relatively large flowers (compared with the size of the plant). Mature flowers stay open for only a few days. The lip is broader than the sepals and petals, and is 3-lobed with fringed keels.

In recent years, a pink flowering *Pleione* has become increasingly popular in Melbourne.

Culture

These ground orchids have small rounded pseudobulbs and deciduous leaves. Many grow well in cold climates, tolerating night temperatures to 10°C (lower when dormant).

Flowers are large and colourful, and provided drainage is good they grow well in pots. A partly shaded position protected from extreme temperatures or cold winds is preferred.

Provide good light, but avoid direct sunlight.

Start feeding with weak liquid fertiliser every two days once a flower shoot is detected.

For best results, repot annually after flowering, and never bury the pseudobulb when planting. Pot only in shallow containers in a mix of equal parts of composted bark, chopped sphagnum and coarse sand.

A healthy and vigorous pseudobulb will produce two new shoots each year, which can be separated after pseudobulbs form at the base of those shoots. The original (older) pseudobulb can be grown on then to produce a second pair of new pseudobulbs. Unlike many other orchids that have pseudobulbs, the Pleione pseudobulb usually lives for only around two years.

Cultivars

P. formosa has mainly pink flowers. The lip is heavily fringed, and has a yellow blotched centre. It flowers in spring.

P. Hookereana has only one leaf, around 9 cm long, on each pseudobulb. The flowers are whitish to rose-flushed, and the lip is brown to purple and yellow.

P. humilis has one leaf, up to 20 cm long, per pseudobulb. Flowers are mainly white with reddish to brownish markings inside the lip. An individual flower can be up to 10 cm across. Over winter, keep the plant in a dry cold position near freezing point, but avoid frost.

P. limprichtii has predominantly pink flowers.

P. maculata has two leaves, up to 20 cm long, per pseudobulb. The petals and sepals that are mainly white, but sometimes have pink stripes. The lip has pink, yellow and purplish markings inside.

P. praecox has two leaves, to 20 cm long, per pseudobulb. The flowers are predominantly rose-purple with white, and a little yellow inside the lip. *P. praecox* is sometimes called 'Mother of the Pleiades'. It requires a definite rest period early winter, after which it flowers before growing leaves.

P. Reichenbachiana has pseudobulbs to 6 cm long, topped with 1-2 leaves to around 6 cm. Flowers are predominantly pale rose to lilac with white margins and a white lip with purplish spots.

P. speciosa has a mainly rich dark purplish-pink, slightly scented, flower. It has yellow or pale ridges inside the lip.

PLEUROTHALLIS

(Abbreviation – Pths.)

This is a close relative of *Masdevallia*, from tropical America.

There are approximately 1000 species, mainly epiphytes, some lithophytes, and occasionally terrestrial plants. Species vary greatly in size from 1 cm to 1 m or more. Stems are either creeping or occur in tufts. A single leaf emerges from each leaf bud. There are no pseudobulbs present. The small flowers occur on a raceme or singly, and may emerge from either the stem axils or rhizomes.

Culture

The culture is similar to that for *Cattleya* or *Masdevallia*.

Pot into a bark mix. Pot up infrequently and with as little root disturbance as possible.

Pleurothallis generally prefer good light, so avoid more than 60-75% shade. The temperature requirements can vary greatly, but there are species suited to a wide range of temperature conditions.

Overall this is a very hardy genus, more susceptible to excessive watering than underwatering. Water only when the plant is in its growth phase.

Most species flower in summer or autumn, though exact flowering times are often difficult to predict.

Large plants can be propagated by division; avoid potting small divisions, which will take a long time to produce flowers.

Cultivars

P. calyptrosepala is a dwarf creeping ground orchid, to 2.5 cm tall. The flowers are yellow with a blackish tip and very small.

P. Ghiesbreghtiana (syn. *P. quadrifida*) is an epiphyte producing a tuft of leaves to 70 cm tall. Flower spikes carry many slightly fragrant small lemon-yellow flowers.

P. grandis has a solitary leathery elliptical leaf, and greenish flowers with red to brown markings on a pendulous stem.

P. immersa forms a cluster of fleshy leaves to 20 cm long, and has green to yellow flowers with brownish markings.

P. macrophylla (syn. *P. Roezlii*) is a robust plant to 50 cm tall with fleshy leaves to 25cm in length. Known as the Widow Orchid, its flower spikes carry many predominantly dark purple flowers, each to around 2.5 cm across.

PTEROSTYLIS (GREENHOODS, MAROONHOODS, RUSTYHOODS)

(Abbreviation – Ptst.)

There are approximately 120 species of these terrestrial orchids, mainly from Australia, but some from surrounding countries; they grow singly or in colonies. Most occur in moist soil in open woodland or close to water courses. Some have adapted to more varied conditions. They die back to small tuberoids in dry, hot summers, then with autumn rain the tuberoids grow afresh. Most produce a rosette of leaves at ground level (anything from 2-20 leaves can be common). A flowering stem growing from the basal rosette can also bear leaves (or leaf-like structures). The dorsal sepals and petals are always joined to create a hooded structure (called the galea), which is characteristic of this genus.

Culture

Some species are quite easy to grow, and will flower in cultivation; others are more difficult. Most do well in a cool greenhouse or shadehouse in a temperate climate.

Keep the soil moist, but not wet, through autumn to spring, and allow the soil to dry out over summer when the plants are dormant; water again in autumn when growth starts.

The growing medium should consist of about 30% eucalypt wood or leaf compost and 70% gravelly or sandy soil.

Cultivation techniques vary according to species. Clump-forming species which multiply quickly are easily propagated by division.

Cultivars

Species are divided into two main groups:

- colony forming – these are generally much easier to grow, because they increase vegetatively; repotting becomes necessary every two years.
- solitary – these orchids are more difficult to grow; they need excellent drainage and potting soil MUST be correct. They are particularly sensitive to over-wet soil.

P. alata (Striped Greenhood) forms a colony. Cultivation is sometimes easy, but some growers have difficulty: this may be due to a failure to match the plants' environmental source. The flowers have prominent dark green or brownish stripes on top, and the flower is 3 cm long. It occurs widely throughout Tasmania and south-eastern Australia.

P. baptistii (King Greenhood) is another colony grower. Flowers are large and translucent, white with green and brown markings, and grow on 40 cm stalks. This is an easy-to-grow Greenhood.

P. concinna (Trim Greenhood) is a rosette-forming orchid with solitary translucent white, green and brown flowers. It is also easy to grow.

P. curta (Blunt Greenhood) is very easy to cultivate. It is a clump-forming orchid with a flowering stem to 30 cm tall. There is normally a single flower, 3.5 cm long, with whitish or green stripes and brownish markings. This species is very widespread, occurring from Queensland to Victoria, Tasmania and South Australia.

P. cycnocephala (Swan Greenhood) produces a rosette of more than six leaves. The 20 cm tall stalk produces numerous small bright green and white flowers. It tends to grow as a solitary specimen but is still considered easy to grow.

P. longifolia (Tall Greenhood) can grow to almost 1 m high, bearing 1-15 white flowers with brown tips. It is solitary in habit, but relatively easy to grow. It occurs widely from south-east Queensland to South Australia and Tasmania.

Pterostylis nana

P. nana (Dwarf Greenhood) develops only green flowers above a stalk that grows to 15 cm. Plants produce a rosette of leaves.

P. nutans (Nodding Greenhood) is clump forming and very easy to cultivate. Its stem grows to 30 cm tall and usually carries a single flower (occasionally two). Flowers are translucent and green-striped. This species is very widespread, growing naturally in a great variety of different habitats.

P. obtusa (Blunt-Tongued Greenhood) grows in colonies and is relatively easy to cultivate. It produces a solitary translucent white flower with brown and green markings.

P. setifera produces semi-translucent flowers with green or light brown markings. It has distinctive bristles on the labellum.

RENANTHERA (FIRE ORCHIDS)

(Abbreviation – Ren.)

Renanthera is closely related to *Vanda*. There are approximately 15 species including epiphytes, lithophytes and occasionally terrestrials. They are native to South East Asia; most are from low elevations and grow in bright light.

The stems are leafy and the roots are almost all aerial. The flower stems are horizontal and many-branched. The flowers can be small or large, and are usually red, sometimes with yellowish tones. Sepals and petals are narrow and spreading, and the lip is small.

Culture

Provide around 50%-70% shade. The soft foliage can burn in this light shade, but flowering may be reduced in heavier shade. Many growers in tropic zones recommend no more than 70% to achieve flowering.

Most species need warm conditions.

Watering can be minimised by ensuring high humidity. In non-humid zones, drenching the plants and roots with water is recommended.

Species and hybrids can be placed directly on exposed tree trunks in lowland tropics and sub-tropic zones. Alternatively they can be grown in clay or wooden slat orchid baskets filled with very chunky/coarse orchid mixture. Some growers use horticultural charcoal, with sphagnum.

Tall flower spikes may need staking.

Spray the medium at the top of the pot with weak liquid fertiliser occasionally when the plant is in its growth phase.

Cultivars

R. coccinea has long climbing stems covered with pale green leaves approximately 6 cm long. Flowers can occur at any time of the year, and are predominantly reddish with white and yellow markings.

R. elangata is an epiphyte that occurs in tropic swamp zones and is terrestrial in grasslands. Flower spikes carry many small yellow flowers with purple and red markings.

R. imschootiana is a species from the Indian highlands, occurring at altitudes to 1500 m. It is relatively cold-hardy. Flowers have broad red lateral sepals with some yellowish spots on other parts.

R. matutina comes from wet mountainous forests in Java and the Philippines. Its flower colour varies but is usually crimson.

R. monachica has strap-like leaves around 12 cm long. Its flowers have long thin sepals and petals, yellowish with red markings. This orchid occurs in grasslands in the Philippines.

R. philippinensis has numerous blood-red scented flowers, 3.5 cm across, on a stalk 60 cm long .

R. Storiei has leaves to 20 cm long and deep red flowers, each 6 cm across, borne on a branching stalk 65 cm long.

Renanthera has been used extensively in breeding with other Vanda-related orchids such as Aerides, Arachnis, Ascocentrum, Doritis, Phalaenopsis, Sarcochilus, and Vanda itself, plus others.

RHYNCHOLAELIA

These plants were once included as *Brassavola*, but are now a separate genus of two species.

Rhyncholaelia orchids are epiphytes native to the hot dry regions of tropical Central America. They tend to grow best outdoors in lightly tropical climates or in warm greenhouses in cool climates.

These orchids tend to produce single flowers with narrow petals, and with an obvious fringed or toothed lip. The single grey-green leaves are leathery and elliptical. Pseudostems are hard-looking and grow up to 20 cm tall.

Culture

These orchids can be treated similarly to *Cattleya*, but with reduced watering, especially in the off-growing season. Do not water excessively at any time.

The plants may be grown on trees, or on a slab, but are generally better in a pot with a coarse medium.

Apply fertiliser only during the growing phase.

Neither species is reported as suited to tropical culture. They seem best grown in warmed greenhouses in sub-tropical or temperate climates.

Cultivars

R. digbyana has the most spectacular flowers of the two species, and as such has been more widely grown. Flowers are large and scented, light green with a fringed lip. The plant needs to be a significant size before it will flower, and requires more light than a *Cattleya*.

R. glauca, although less commonly grown, does merit attention. Its scented flowers have green to white or lavender petals, with a cream lip spotted and striped with red.

These plants are often used as a parent in cross-pollination with *Cattleya*, for the purpose of introducing the fringed lip.

Sarcochilus

(Abbreviation – Sarco.)

Sarcochilus is closely related to *Vanda*. There are approximately 20 species including epiphytes and lithophytes, with great variation in characteristics. They are native to South East Asia and Australia.

Stems are short or absent, and no pseudobulbs are present. Leaves are oblong or absent. Flowers occur on a pendulant raceme and are commonly small; they are variable in colour from green to white or pink. Some have a pleasant fragrance.

Culture

Cultural requirements vary according to species, and their original habitats.

Tropical species require temperature conditions similar to those for *Phalaenopsis*. The cooler growing species (mainly from Australia) need temperatures of 13°C minimum (and some moisture) over winter to do well. Leafless species need a definite rest period when they are dormant. Species with hard textured leaves require less watering in winter.

Many of the epiphytes are specific to a small range of host trees, so ideally the same type of tree should be provided for a particular orchid to attach to.

Propagate as for *Vanda*; but success may be elusive.

Cultivars

S. Ceciliae is an Australian native. Its roots rarely grow into the potting medium, but cover the surface only. In nature it grows over the surface of moss-covered rocks; so supply chunks of rock (e.g. sandstone) in the potting medium, and roots may attach to them. This species has pinkish flowers in autumn to early winter.

S. falcatus is a small Australian native with broad, almost oval, leaves, and white or cream to pink fragrant flowers.

S. Hartmannii is perhaps the strongest growing species in cultivation. It commonly produces thick waxy red and white flowers, but there are several varieties with other colours. This species is prized for its floral display.

S. luniferus is a small epiphyte with lots of aerial roots. These photosynthesise, to supplement a scarcity of leaves. Flowers are red-orange with yellow margins.

S. Mannii has drooping stems to 30 cm long, occasionally branching, with leathery leaves around 10 cm long. The tiny flowers, less than 1 cm across, are pale pink with crimson markings.

S. olivaceus is a small epiphyte with fragrant lime-green flowers. Up to 20 flowers have been known to occur on the raceme. This orchid normally carries only four leaves.

S. roseus is a semi-erect lithophyte with thick leaves and sprays of rosy pink flowers 25 cm tall.

Sophronitis

(Abbreviation – Soph.)

These orchids are related closely to *Cattleya*, and come mainly from Brazil. There are approximately eight species, all small epiphytes, each plant carrying only one leathery leaf per pseudobulb. A flower stem in most species has only one flower.

Culture

Use a potting medium similar to that which is suitable for *Cattleya*, but with particle sizes a little finer. Repot in spring as soon as new growth starts.

Sophronitis like summer temperatures suitable for *Odontoglossum*, whereas winter minimums should not be below 13°C.

Water the plants all year to keep them moist, and only slightly reduce watering in winter. Good drainage is very important.

Shade the orchids over summer, but decrease the level of shade in cooler months, particularly if the plants are growing in temperate climates. Better flower colour is achieved in brighter light.

Fertilise every three weeks during the growing stage with general liquid fertiliser at 25-50% recommended strength.

Propagate by dividing the branching rhizomes.

Cultivars

S. brevipedunculata produces bold rich red flowers from the single-leaved pseudobulb.

S. cernua produces cylindrical pseudobulbs just over 1 cm long, a grey-green leaf around 2.5 cm, and two or three tiny reddish flowers, each with a lip that is paler at the base.

S. coccinea (syn. *S. grandiflora*) is perhaps the most commonly grown species. It is a small orchid that likes cool shade, moderate temperatures and a well-drained medium; it needs to be regularly watered all year (do not allow a dormant period). Flowers can vary from 3-8 cm across, and are generally scarlet with yellowish-red, and a streaked lip. For optimum flowering provide 80-85% humidity all year, and bright light (but not direct sun).

S. Lowii (syn. *S. coccinea* var. *Lowii*) is smaller than *S. coccinea*, and has yellow flowers.

S. violacea has pseudobulbs to 2.5 cm long, leaves to 6 cm and purplish flowers in winter.

Hybrids

Sophronitis are hybridised with *Laeliocattleya* to produce *Sophrolaeliocattleya* (*Slc.*) hybrids (see under *Cattleya*).

Spathoglottis

(Abbreviation – Spa.)

There are around 45 species of these terrestrial orchids from tropical countries. They produce corm-like pseudobulbs on a creeping rhizome. Between one and five leaves can arise from each pseudobulb; these are often grass-like. Some species are deciduous (dying back for a season each year).

There are 3-12 or more flowers on a spike. Flower colours vary among species from white to pinks and purples.

Culture

Most species are considered warm-climate orchids. They are similar to *Calanthe*, but generally have narrower leaves with a longer leaf stalk.

Shade is particularly important for the first month after planting. When growing these orchids in a greenhouse 60-75% shade is ideal for plants at any stage of growth. Always avoid direct sun.

Spathoglottis prefer minimum temperatures of 15°C or higher.

They respond well to feeding.

In South East Asia, a beetle pest can be a problem, so routine spraying may be necessary here.

Grow in a freely draining potting medium that remains moist between waterings, but not wet. Avoid overwatering, even in the tropics. Water well, then allow the plant to become almost totally dry before watering again. Whether you grow the plants in soil or in pots, always ensure very good drainage, and if necessary, grow them in raised beds. These orchids grow well as border plants in shaded or semi-shaded areas and are frequently planted in garden beds in tropical areas.

Cultivars

S. aurea produces pseudobulbs to 20 cm tall, with leaves to 90 cm long; they are tinged with purple. Rich yellow flowers with reddish markings can reach 8 cm across. *S. aurea* can be difficult to cultivate.

S. kimballiana is similar to *S. aurea*, but has more golden yellow colour in the flowers.

S. lobbii (syn. *S. affinis*) is a deciduous species, with sulphur-yellow flowers.

S. pacifica is a terrestrial orchid from the forests of tropical South Pacific Islands. The flowers are mainly pale lavender to pink.

S. papuana comes from Papua New Guinea, and produces a succession of small carmine-rose flowers on tall slender spikes for several months each year.

S. pauliniae has pseudobulbs to 5 cm with large pleated leaves to 1.8 m long. Flower stems grow to 1.2 m tall and can carry up to 25 flowers (usually less). The self-pollinating flowers are usually white to dark red.

S. plicata is the most common terrestrial orchid in Malaysian gardens. Its leaves grow to 45 cm long, and 5-7 cm wide, and the flower clusters are commonly purple. There are also white- or mauve-flowering varieties available.

S. Singapore Giant has been produced by crossing different varieties of *S. plicata*. This is a very attractive free-flowering variety with flower spikes to 1 m tall.

Hybrids

S. aurea × *S. plicata*: produce hybrids with very attractive yellow flowers; some also have some mauve or purple in the flower.

Spa. Dwarf Legion is an interspecies hybrid with flowers in various shades of pink. It is 50% *S. tomentosa*, 25% *S. Parsonii* and 25% *S. Primrose*.

Bangkok Yellow Hybrids are yellow-flowering plants bred in Bangkok from *S. kimballiana* and other varieties.

THELYMITRA (SUN ORCHIDS)

(Abbreviation – Thel.)

There are approximately 45 species of Sun Orchids, mostly Australian deciduous terrestrial species.

They come mainly from temperate areas, though there are some tropical species. Most grow as scattered individual plants or in small groups; a few grow in larger colonies. They commonly prefer well-drained loamy soils, though some grow in other types. *Thelymitra* frequently occur in open woodland or heathland.

All have a single upright leaf growing from the base. Flowers are relatively simple, but generally very colourful (no lip as in most other orchids). The most common flower colour is a shade of bright blue (a rare colour amongst orchids), though there are many variations, including shades of yellow, pink and red.

Culture

Some species adapt well to cultivation while others (often the more desirable types) are very difficult to grow.

Allow potting mix to dry out while the plants are dormant over summer. Recommence watering at the first sign of autumn growth.

Look closely at the natural conditions of the particular species you wish to grow, and mimic these; for example, water more if the species occurs naturally in wetter soil. Some grow naturally in very wet sites and can even be grown with their pot standing in a saucer of water.

Propagation is often reasonably easy by sprinkling seed around the base of a parent plant.

Cultivars

T. antennifera (Lemon Orchid, Rabbit's Ears) is a particularly common and widespread species from Victoria, South Australia, Tasmania and Western

Australia. It produces a flower stem 25 cm tall, which holds 1-3 lemon-scented and yellow flowers. This species can be difficult to maintain in culture.

T. arenaria has pale blue flowers with a yellow column on 35 cm stalks. It is easy to grow in temperate districts.

T. cyanea (Veined Blue Orchid) has a flower stem to 50 cm tall, bearing 1-6 variable, but normally bright blue, flowers with darker veins. It occurs naturally in south-eastern Australia and New Zealand, usually growing amongst grass in sub-alpine habitats. Keep moist (it grows best in a pot of sphagnum or peat moss standing in water).

T. × *irregularis* (Crested Sun Orchid) is a natural hybrid with pink flowers with darker spots.

T. nuda is one of the most widespread species, occurring throughout most of eastern and southern Australia, in forests, open woodland and heathland. Some forms are scented, and some can be cultivated with relative ease. The flower stem reaches 60 cm tall and carries 2-20 flowers, usually blue, but sometimes in other colours. Each flower is 2-4 cm across.

T. pauciflora (Slender Sun Orchid) is a widespread orchid with great flower and habitat diversity. The flowers are, however, usually in shades of blue.

VANDA

(Abbreviation – V.)

Vanda's closely related genera include *Phalaenopsis*, *Doritis*, *Aranda* and *Ascocendra*. There are approximately 60 species of these epiphytes from tropical Asia.

Leaves occur in opposite rows up tall stems, with the base of the leaf sheathing the stem. Leaves are normally thick, leathery or fleshy. These orchids have a climbing habit.

Most have medium to large flowers, usually attractive and frequently fragrant.

Culture

While cultural treatment of each cultivar is best matched to its natural origin, the following generally applies.

Water frequently when growing, but as growth slows water sparingly, particularly over winter. Though some species will tolerate temperatures as low as 10°C over winter, others deteriorate rapidly at temperatures below 20°C.

Shade is essential over summer, the amount depending on the texture and tenderness of foliage. A level of 50% shade is ideal, though in winter narrow-leaved vandaceous plants can tolerate more sunlight. Broader strap-leaved types still need 50% shade, even in winter. In cooler climates, cultivars with harder more leathery leaves may benefit from being exposed to extra light in autumn.

Ventilation is important, but cold draughts must be avoided.

Thrip can be a problem, attacking flowers and flower buds, so routine spraying may be necessary.

White aerial roots develop on the stems as they grow upwards. When the stems have produced a good growth of these, sections of stem can then be taken as stem cuttings – roots can be left on such cuttings, but handle them gently when you are potting up.

Propagation of taller climbing cultivars can easily be done by simply removing a section of healthy growth with some aerial roots still attached.

Cultivars

Vanda are often grouped according to their leaf type:

- terete: these have leaves that are round in cross section, usually with a point at the tip.
- strap-leaved: these have flattened leaves arranged opposite each other in a single plane up a stem.
- semi-terete: these are flattened cylindrical leaves, usually hybrids produced by breeding terete and strap types together. They are generally easier to grow than terete types.

V. Besoni tolerates much higher temperatures than many others. It has yellowish fragrant flowers with a white to rose-purple lip. It has strap leaves.

V. coerulea (Blue Orchid) is one of the most spectacular cultivars, with leathery strap leaves, and stems climbing to 80 cm tall. Flowers are light to dark blue, frequently with purplish markings. It is often difficult to grow. This species needs strong light, particularly if temperatures and humidity are lower. Some varieties tolerate temperatures as low as 8°C in winter.

V. Denisoniana grows naturally at average temperatures of 20-25°C. It has a white flower. It produces large strap leaves to 30 cm or longer.

V. Hookeriana has terete foliage and can grow to 2 m tall. Flowers are mainly purple. It can be difficult to cultivate and is less vigorous than some species. It needs more water and humidity than some, and in mild climates may require heating all year; but it can flower continuously if grown well.

V. Sanderiana has variable pink and brown flowers. It requires minimum night temperatures of 15°C, but grows better at warmer temperatures. Leaves are large, strap-shaped and leathery.

V. teres has terete leaves. It requires more light than most other *Vanda*; almost full sun is ideal. It also needs a period of dryish weather to stimulate flowering (hence it does not flower well in continually humid tropical conditions). The flowers are rose to white or pale orange.

V. tricolor is a strap-leaved type that will tolerate very cold conditions but not frost. Its flowers are white and maroon, spotted in parts. There are various named cultivars with colour variations.

V. watsonnii requires conditions similar to Odontoglossums. Its flowers are white with a fringed lip.

Hybrids

Many hybrids have been heavily based on *V. sanderiana* and *V. coerulea*.

New terete hybrid *Vanda* have been produced from mainly terete species, sometimes crossed with non-terete. Common parents of this group include *V. hookeriana*, *V. tricuspidata* and *V. teres*.

V. Miss Joaquim is a hybrid of *V. teres* × *V. hookeriana*. It has large pink flowers with some orange in the centre, and is probably the most commonly grown *Vanda* in Malaysia, where it can grow to around 1 m tall in full sun; it is very free flowering.

Vandanthe – *Vanda sanderiana* was renamed *Euanthe sanderiana* in 1914. *Vanda* hybrids with this plant as a parent are known as 'Vandanthe'.

Vandanthe rothschildiana (i.e. *Vanda coerulea* × *Euanthe sanderiana*) develops orange-red spotted flowers.

Vandaenopsis – these are hybrids of *Vanda* and *Phalaenopsis*.

Aranda – hybrids with *Arachnis* and *Vanda*.

Hybrids between *Vanda* and *Rhynchostylis* or *Renanthera* are also grown.

VANILLA

Vanilla is closely related to *Phaius*. There are approximately 60 to 70 species with a generally climbing habit, and often with long branching stems. Some are leafless, some have fleshy or leathery leaves. They can be terrestrial or become epiphytic. If all contact is broken between the ground and a climbing plant, it can still thrive attached to the tree it is climbing. Some species have relatively few flowers; others flower many more.

The species *V. planifolia* (syn. *V. fragrans*) is grown for the elongated seed pods, known as 'vanilla beans', some of which yield the vanilla extract used as a flavouring. The West Indian Vanilla (*V. pompona*) and *V. tahitensis* are alternative species which can be cultivated as a secondary source of commercial vanilla extract.

These and other species are also grown as an ornamental in some tropical countries.

Vanilla orchid

Culture

For good results *Vanilla* vines need a warm moist tropic climate, and an annual rainfall of 190-250 cm (75-100 in). These orchids respond well to rich, organic soils, 30-50% shade and protection from wind.

Commercially grown plantings are hand pollinated to ensure a high yield of beans.

Vanilla vines are commonly cultivated on quick-growing shade trees grown specifically for that purpose, and planted at least nine months before the vines. The vanilla vine has to be supported over low branches within your reach. Prune the trees to give several lateral branches and to give easy access between the rows of trees. Prune once a year to regulate the shade. Too much shade (when grass does not grow well) weakens the vine and encourages disease. As you prune, mulch pruned stems around the plant.

The roots should be kept moist but not over-wet. Mulching is valuable.

The vanilla vine is shallow- or surface-rooted and the soil surface around it must be kept moist and not disturbed by weeding. Spread mulch around the plant leaving a space of 10-15 cm from the vine's base. This uncovered space can be filled continually with vegetable matter (e.g. kitchen scraps), which composts readily, to provide nutrients for the *Vanilla* plant. Water frequently during dry weather.

Before planting prepare the site by weeding, digging and mulching.

Select only healthy vines for planting, and cut them to a length of about 1 m. Shorter lengths take longer to flower. Hang cuttings in a cool place, preferably 10-15 days under shade before planting.

Plant vines 1.5-2.5 m apart in a row and leave a 3 m space between each row.

Plant one vine by each of the shade trees which have already been planted (as above). Remove 2-3 leaves from the base of the vine and lay it at a shallow depth in the soil, leaving the end tip 1 cm above the ground.

Train the growing tip of the vine up the shade tree and tie it loosely with twine. Vines are trained to keep the flowers within reach for pollination and harvesting.

Young vines are brittle, so be cautious. A long *Vanilla* vine can be trained by looping it over a support and back to the soil. This produces more roots, providing extra support, a better supply of nutrients, and an extension of the of the planting's lifespan if the original root system weakens and dies out.

The *Vanilla* vine flowers in the third year after planting. A healthy developed vine produces 100-400 pale yellow flowers over a 3-4 month period every year. The flowers open in the morning and close in the afternoon.

NOTE – Flowers must be hand pollinated to produce beans or pods.

Hand pollinate only 8-10 flowers on each flower spike, in the morning when the flowers open (8 a.m. till noon). Select only 4-6 pods in every cluster of 100-150 vines, from four years old to full maturity. Don't pollinate unhealthy vines, as it can further weaken the plant.

Beans grow to 15-25 cm long. Longer beans fetch the highest price. The beans mature in 7-9 months and are picked just before ripening as the colour starts to change from green to yellow. If they are harvested at this stage the beans can split.

ZYGOPETALUM

(Abbreviation – Z.)

There are approximately 20 species that are either, or both, epiphytes or terrestrials, from Central and South America. They are not particularly suited to hot humid tropics or sub-tropics. They have ovoid pseudobulbs, each of which has one or two leaves which are lanceolate in shape. Foliage of most species is glossy and becomes deciduous when mature. *Zygopetalum* flowers appear on erect racemes which grow from the base of the pseudobulbs. There can be a few or many flowers on a raceme. They are generally long-lasting, and can be small or large, but either way, are conspicuous, often with vivid markings.

Culture

Zygopetalum need reasonably good light, so avoid heavy shade (60% is adequate). Good ventilation is also important.

Many will grow under shade cloth in cool temperate areas (e.g. Melbourne) if they are not exposed to frost.

Use the same potting medium as for *Cymbidium*. When potting be careful with the plant's brittle roots to avoid breaking them. Do not overpot, but still allow ample room for expansion to minimise the need for frequent handling.

Zygopetalum

Apply slow release organic fertiliser to the surface of the potting medium at the start of the growing season. Feed frequently with medium doses of fertiliser while the plants are in growth.

Keep moist during the growth stage, but water sparingly at other times.

Cultivars

Z. intermedium is a commonly grown species, with flower spikes to 70 cm long in winter. Flowers are fragrant, and greenish with brownish blotches and a white and violet lip. Many growers find this species difficult to distinguish from *Z. mackayii*. This cultivar rarely produces more than six flowers on a stem.

Z. mackayii is similar to *Z. intermedium*, but with slight differences (e.g. the lip is smooth on *Z. mackayii*, while it is covered with hairs or fur on *Z. intermedium;* Z. *mackayii* commonly produces around 10 flowers on a stem). *Z. mackayii* is relatively hardy, growing well with minimum temperatures to 10°C; most like it warmer.

Z. maxillare produces up to eight flowers on a stem. It has a creeping habit with well-spaced pseudobulbs, and waxy fragrant flowers. It needs hot conditions.

Hybrids

There are many registered *Zygopetalum* hybrids, and the species listed above are common species.

Some of the original hybridisation was poorly documented (or researched). This has led to uncertainty as to the parentage of some hybrids; in fact some plants sold as *Zygopetalum* might not even be that. *Zygopetallum* hybridises freely with two other genera: *Mendoncella* (syn. *Galeottia*) and *Pabstia* (hybrids sometimes called *Zygopabstia*).

further information

DISTANCE EDUCATION COURSES

The author of this book conducts a large number of correspondence courses through the Australian Correspondence Schools including Orchid Culture (Ht416) and Cut Flower Orchids (Ht314). Further information can be obtained from:

Australian Correspondence Schools
PO Box 2092, Nerang DC, Qld, 4211
Ph: (07) 5530 4855 Fax: (07) 5525 1728
Email: admin@acs.edu.au

or

264 Swansea Rd, Lilydale, Vic, 3140
Ph: (03) 9736 1882 Fax: (03) 9736 4034
Email: vic@acs.edu.au
Website: http://www.acs.edu.au

For more information on orchids consult the internet e-zine at www.acsgarden.com

MAGAZINES

Australian Orchid Review
14 McGill St, Lewisham, NSW, 2049
Ph (02) 9560 6166

Australian Horticulture
PO Box 254, Moonee Ponds, Vic, 3039
Ph 1300 – 131 095 (within Australia)

Flower Link
PO Box 1256, Castle Hill, NSW, 2154

The Orchid Review
New Gate Farm, Cotchey Lane, Stour Provost, Gillingham, Dorset, SP85LT, UK

American Orchid Society Bulletin
American Orchid Society, Dept AOR, 6000 South Olive Ave, West Palm Beach, Florida, 33405, USA

Indian Orchid Journal
'Ganesh Villa', Kalimpong, 734301, West Bengal, India

AUSTRALIAN ORCHID SOCIETIES

(Secretaries)

VIC: 1 Tynan St, West Preston, Vic, 3072. Ph (03) 9478 9764

NSW: PO Box 333, Beverly Hills, NSW, 2209. Ph (02) 9759 5948

QLD: PO Box 126BC, Browns Plains, Qld, 4118. Ph (07) 3800 3213

SA: GPO Box 730, Adelaide, SA, 5001. Ph (03) 8336 3822

WA: PO Box 58, Como, WA, 6152. Ph (08) 9367 9306

TAS: 166 Carella St, Howrah, Tas, 7018. Ph (03) 6247 9636

NT: PO Box 38493, Winnellie, NT, 5789. Ph (08) 8927 4148

ACT: GPO Box 613, Canberra, ACT, 2601. Ph (02) 6251 6621

Glossary

Axil – the angle between the upper side of a leaf and the stem to which it is attached

Axillary – located at the axil of a leaf (i.e. axillary bud)

Basal – at the base of the plant

Bulb – in common usage it usually refers to any plant which has underground (or close to ground level) parts modified for storage, e.g. swollen stem or root, etc.; some orchids have parts like this (e.g. swollen sections at the base of cymbidium leaves are called 'pseudobulbs'); in botanical terms, it refers to a modified underground bud or stem

Clavate – club-shaped, with the thickest part usually at the top

Corolla – the envelopes that surround the flower, or reproductive parts, of a plant

Cultivar – a variety of plant that has been produced only under cultivation

Dorsal – relating to the surface away from the axis or stem

Epiphyte – a plant which grows above the ground, usually attached to another plant or tree trunk; they are non-parasitic, using the other plant only for support

Exotic – plant which is not indigenous (i.e. has been introduced from some other country)

Genus – the first botanical name given to a plant; begins with a capital letter and is written in italics

Hybrid – plant which has resulted from an artificial cross-breeding of two different plants, usually two different species, though many orchids are actually hybrids between different genera

Indigenous – native to a particular area or country; also referred to as native

Intergeneric hybrid – plant resulting from an artificial cross-breeding of two plants within the same species but of different genera; orchid hybrids are specified as intergeneric or interspecies because of the large number of hybrids that occur

Interspecies hybrid – plant resulting from an artificial cross-breeding of two plants of different species; orchid hybrids are specified as interspecies (rather than just 'hybrid') because of the large number and combinations of interbreeding that occur

Labellum – the lip of a flower; specifically refers to the flowers in the Orchidaceae family

Lateral – at the side

Linear – nearly or definitely parallel; like a blade of grass

Lip – modified petal; also known as labellum

Lithophyte – a plant which grows attached to the surface of a rock, absorbing its nourishment from the atmosphere and decomposing leaf debris

Lobed – usually referring to a leaf or petal, it is the clefts or sinuses dividing the margin or edge of the leaf; the division is to no more than half of the leaf

Mycorrhiza – a non-pathogenic association of a fungus with the roots of certain plants

Native – plant which is indigenous to a particular country (i.e. an Australian native is a plant which occurs naturally in Australia)

Ovoid – slightly oval in shape, similar to an egg

Panicle – a compound raceme; any loose diversely branching flower cluster

Paniculate – borne in a panicle or looking very similar to a panicle

Peduncle – orchid's flower stalk

Perianth – collective term for the corolla and calyx, whether these are distinct from each other or undifferentiated

Petal – separate, showy part of a corolla

Petiole- the stalk by which the leaf is attached to the stem

Photosynthesis – the process by which plants utilise sunlight to create stored energy within the leaves

Pseudobulb – a thick, above-ground stem that occurs in some types of orchids

Raceme – a kind of flowering shoot with the flowers occurring on the main axis or stalk

Racemose – a flowering shoot (inflorescence) which is monopodial (has no rhizomes or pseudobulbs) and flowers on the main stalk; includes raceme, umbel, spike and panicle flowers

Rhizome – a stem that grows horizontally, normally at or below ground level

Scape – a peduncle or flower stalk that has no foliage leaves; can have scales or bracts

Sepal – part of the calyx, or outer covering of the flower

Sessile – attached by the base, as a leaf or flower with no stalk

Species – refers to the second botanical name given to a plant; normally written in italics and with first letter in lower case

Stolon – a stem that grows horizontally, normally above ground level

Sympodial – creeping horizontal stem that produces pseudobulbs from lateral buds

Terete – a tapering cylinder

Terrestrial – a plant which grows in the soil

Variety – a name given to a plant that is identified as a subgroup to a species; written down in single quotation marks

Venation – the pattern or lay-out of veins in a leaf

Virus – highly infectious organism that causes harm to the vigour of the plant

Index